Praise for Ann Van Eron and *Open Stance*

"As an executive coach, I know the first step to great leadership is being open to receiving feedback, understanding your team's perspective, and staying open-minded to new ideas and suggestions. Ann has done a masterful job of walking readers through the process of staying open and reflective, allowing you to more easily pivot and respond to any circumstance. A critical book for every leader!"

— Marshall Goldsmith, *New York Times* #1 Bestselling Author of *Triggers*, *Mojo*, and *What Got You Here Won't Get You There* Thinkers 50 #1 Executive Coach and only two-time #1 Leadership Thinker in the world

"Being open and adapting to the ever-changing environment is essential for success today. Our leaders are more resilient and are creating enhanced engagement with the Open Stance mindset and skills. Open Stance Leadership and the OASIS Conversations courses have been valuable for shifting to a collaborative culture. We are grateful to Ann Van Eron and her work with our organization. This book is essential for anyone who desires to create more influential, positive, and productive relationships and experience greater possibility."

— Sherif Kamel, Senior Vice President, CVS Health

"Ann Van Eron's latest book, *Open Stance: Thriving Amid Differences and Uncertainty,* is brilliant in its conception, timeliness, and simplicity! On the heels of arguably the most complex and daunting challenges of our lifetime, Van Eron offers a very simple refuge—be open! Embodying an *open stance* is both an art and a lifelong commitment to become your best self. This gem of a book is essentially a deep inner dialogue, examining heart and mind to build the spiritual muscle to engage wholeheartedly with the world. It calls on each of us to be the intention for peace and connection that we so desperately need. The promise therein cannot be overestimated!"

— Kathleen FitzSimons, PhD, Executive Coach, KathleenFitzSimonsConsulting, Inc.

"During these complex and unpredictable times, Ann Van Eron has written a book that has us look into the way we think and the resulting impact that

thinking has on the stress and pressure we feel. She offers a model for open thinking backed with science that can be used as a tool to overcome our predetermined mindset traps. Certainly, timely and useful for all."
— Sunita Holzer, EVP, Chief Human Resources Officer, Versik Analytics (previously CHRO with Realogy, Computer Sciences Corporation, Chubb, American Express, and GE Capital)

"Ann Van Eron has done it again in her second book! The Open Stance process supports enhanced awareness of ourselves in order to positively influence our interactions. The process is invaluable in creating and changing cultures. I wish I could have introduced this book to my social work students and colleagues throughout my years of teaching and practice."
— Dolores G. Norton, PhD, Samuel Deutsch Professor Emerita, The University of Chicago

"Ann Van Eron captures the need for centering ourselves in the midst of leadership challenges and provides us the most accessible of methods - our bodies - for reminding ourselves to be at our best. When we are fully present, sensing and not judging, we can be truly open. The wisdom we need is within us. With practice, we share our open stance with others for more trust and better outcomes in any interaction. We need more of this right now."
— Kelly Wojda, Global Learning & Development Director, Caterpillar Inc.

"Ann Van Eron's clarion call for an 'open stance' in today's divided America is a powerful unifying concept. Individuals need to seek out opportunities to help others at work, in their family, and within their local community. Open stance thinking is an antidote to the tribalism and closed mindedness weakening our nation. The future can be bright if we adopt an open mindset to address both personal concerns and societal controversies."
— Edward E. Gordon, PhD, Author of *Future Jobs: Solving the Employment and Skills Crisis* and President, Imperial Consulting Corporation

"Being open is such an essential quality in today's world where each of us face increasing levels of volatility, uncertainty, complexity, and ambiguity in our lives and careers. We need to be open to so many things—open to life, to our feelings, our perceptions, our pain and fears, being wrong, new ideas, changes, etc. Ann's book is a wonderful guide exploring how and why

each of us must invest time in creating as much openness as possible in our lives—both at home and work. She shares some really helpful questions that we can ask ourselves to deepen our self-reflection on being more open. You will particularly find valuable her open stance postures framework about being open-minded, open-hearted, open-centered, and open-handed!"
— Nigel Cumberland, Best-Selling Author of *100 Things Successful People Do* and Award-Winning Executive Coach and Facilitator

"In *Open Stance*, Ann Van Eron provides a practical and powerful method that synthesizes research and best practices for shifting from distracting emotions to a full-body sense of possibility and connection to the beautiful essence of life. The approach is elegant and easy to use. It is a nice complement to her previous book on how to have conversations that help others shift perspective. It is clear that Ann loves to bring joy to the world from her heart."
— Dr. Marcia Reynolds, Author of *Outsmart Your Brain* and President of Covisioning

"By writing a clear and challenging book that couldn't be more timely and on the mark, Ann Van Eron has done it again. It is one thing to want to be open, yet quite another to know how to make the shift from closed to being open, that is, curious, compassionate, courageous, and kind—the key components of actually becoming open. Thank you, Ann, for once again showing us the way to be more of who we can be."
— W. Warner Burke, PhD, Professor of Psychology and Education, Teachers College, Columbia University

"*Open Stance* crystallizes the essence of what is needed to be resilient and thrive in our increasingly uncertain times. In this practical book, Dr. Van Eron elegantly articulates what it means to choose to be open *(i.e., being present, receptive, curious, and anticipating possibilities)* versus closed *(ungrounded, judgmental, stressed, reactive)* and offers a simple framework with actionable skills for helping oneself get to a more open state. This is, indeed, a valuable book for our era!"
— Nisha Advani, PhD, Executive Coach and Consultant, Former Head of Executive Talent and Organization Development, Genentech

"Ann Van Eron is a world-renowned expert in teaching people to communicate in a way that fosters understanding and connection. Her new book, *Open*

Stance: Thriving Amid Differences and Uncertainty, builds on her earlier work by offering readers specific guidance in how to become more open and receptive to the world around them. Linking together neuropsychological research with behavioral techniques, she has created a model for how to live with resilience, optimism, courage, and compassion."

— Gail Golden, PhD, Author of *Curating Your Life*, Executive Coach

"*Open Stance: Thriving Amid Differences and Uncertainty* is a simple yet profound user's guide for living an impactful, successful life. It does not require working harder or smarter. Rather, it offers a clear explanation and simple tools for becoming a better leader, employee, partner, parent, and human being. Ann Van Eron's writing is that rare combination of easy to understand and inspiring. I found myself feeling more calm and joyful just by reading this book!"

— Laurie Zuckerman, President, Zuckerman Consulting Group, Inc.

"In this time of great division in our world, Ann Van Eron shows us how to sharpen the critical skills needed to depolarize difficult situations. With clarity and wisdom, Ann guides us to respect our fears and the choice to *shift* into an Open Stance. This powerful *shift* in both mindset and body readies us to courageously build bridges across the challenging divides we are faced with everyday. Often the broader perspective gained in a strong Open Stance leads to taking actions that make a difference, a difference that we so long for in today's world."

— Pat Ruzich, Ruzich Consulting, High-Performance Coaching

"In *Open Stance*, Ann invites the reader into an experience that activates a shift in mindset, promising possibility, and opportunity, through openness and awareness. Her expertise as a researcher, certified master coach, and accomplished consultant bring credibility and integrity to an individual way of being where resilience, wellbeing, and flourishing are present. Her book is an unselfish gift that helps to make the world a better place."
— Diane Rogers, Author of *Leading hArtfully: The Art of Leading Through Your Heart to Discover the Best in Others*, President of Contagious Change

"More powerful, effective leadership, parenting and influence? This is what we gain from following the distilled easy-to-remember three steps in Dr. Ann Van Eron's latest book *Open Stance: Thriving Amid Differences and*

Uncertainty. Based on her expertise from decades of study and real-world global practice, the book meets us at any level—from a streamlined overview to the pertinent details of how our physiology, nervous system, and brain work. I've been benefiting from her thought leadership for years, and this book sustains and expands those benefits."

— Marie Meade, MBA, Founder, HWP-You.com
(Healthy Wealthy Perennial, LLC)

"When I learned from Ann that openness is contagious, I tried it out with my team at work. Pretty soon, others on my team had adopted an open mindset and were asking me how I had developed mine. The culture of openness that began with just my team spread throughout multiple teams of my company, including leaders, and now Ann's OASIS model is used at my workplace, and I teach seminars to other teams at my office that involve her techniques to adopt an open mindset. *Open Stance* has encouraged me to expand my personal practice of adopting an open mindset. In particular, the practice of being open-minded and developing curiosity about others, as explained in the book, has helped me develop my relationships at work."

— Kevin Welcher, Senior Web Developer, WillowTree

"The practices Ann teaches in *Open Stance* have helped me to adopt an open mindset in every sphere of my life, leading to happier interactions with family, friends, and coworkers, and more inner fulfillment also. I now seek out opportunities to be open and have gained new friends where I did not expect to. I also have developed a personal practice using Ann's open mindset stances when I just cannot seem to be in an open state. My relationships are better than they have ever been. The result is a richness and sense of harmony in my life."

— Natasha Richter, Open Stance Course Participant

"Ann Van Eron's Open Stance and OASIS Conversations Courses are invaluable programs to give leaders the critical skills, abilities, and tools vital to adapting to the ever-changing business environment, and to bringing out the best in themselves and others. No matter how excellent your formal education or subject matter expertise is, business always comes down to judgment calls, relationships, and conversations with others. Most people have had no training in conversation skills or how to manage oneself to shift to be open in the moment to what is in front of us. *OASIS Conversations* gives people a wonderful model to explore any challenging issue through how you have a conversation. *Open Stance* provides a way to shift one's attention and being to make the most out of the current moment. I highly recommend the programs and Ann's books on these topics to anyone who works with others. (And that would be most of us!)"

— Jackie Sloane, Executive Coach,
CEO, Sloane Communications

"For all people who strive for excellence and making a difference in the world, the challenge is to understand how their approach to engaging with others affects all their activities. Ann Van Eron's distinction between open and closed mindsets helps all readers in active self-reflection and creative self-organization to engage in a more open, receptive, and activated stance of possibility."

— Dorothy E. Siminovitch, PhD, MCC, Author of
A Gestalt Coaching Primer: The Path Toward Awareness IQ,
Founder of Gestalt Center for Coaching

"I am so grateful to Ann Van Eron for writing *Open Stance*. I have always considered myself an open-minded person, but this book made me realize just how often I am closed off to people and ideas and how much more beneficial my life could be if I opened myself more to the possibilities. I have found the practices she offers are invaluable for making the shift to being even more open than I was. I'm more excited about my future and the future of my relationships after reading and applying this book. Thank you, Ann."

— Tyler R. Tichelaar, PhD, Award-Winning
Author of *Narrow Lives* and *The Best Place*

OPEN STANCE
Thriving Amid Differences and Uncertainty

Ann Van Eron, PhD
Creator of the OASIS Conversations Process

Open Stance: Thriving Amid Differences and Uncertainty

Copyright © 2022 by Ann Van Eron.

Published by: Open View Press

All Rights Reserved. No part of this book may be used or reproduced in any manner whatsoever without the expressed written permission of the author.

Address all inquiries to:

Ann Van Eron

312-856-1155

Ann@Potentials.com

www.Potentials.com

ISBN: 978-0-9975136-3-9

E-book ISBN: 978-0-9975136-2-2

Library of Congress Control Number: 2021918601

Editor: Tyler Tichelaar, Superior Book Productions

Cover Design: Joseph Sola-Sole

Interior Book Layout: Larry Alexander, Superior Book Productions

Cover photo from 123rf.com

Every attempt has been made to source properly all quotes.

For Joyelle, leaders, parents, and others who inspire.
May we each be open-minded and take an open stance to enjoy life, and through our presence and action, make the world better for all.

Acknowledgments

I AM DEEPLY GRATEFUL TO MY executive coaching and corporate clients for exploring the Open Stance and the OASIS Conversations processes. I have learned much from each of you and appreciate your openness to learn and practice the Open Stance postures. Thank you for sharing your experience of building the mental fitness of being open.

Thank you to those who are a part of the OASIS and Open Stance Community who are committed to sharing these concepts to enhance positive and productive relationships and co-created solutions.

Thank you to all the authors who are cited in this book, as well as many more who have influenced my work. I am deeply grateful to be active in global organization development and executive coaching. I am continually learning and welcome contributing to the field.

Many thanks to my colleagues and friends who have supported me, the birth of this book, and the corresponding Open Stance Leadership Course and the OASIS Conversations Course. Special thanks to Natasha Richter, Kathleen FitzSimons, Mary Trefry, and Kevin Van Eron for your support on this journey and for reading the book and sharing your insights. Thanks to Tyler Tichelaar for your editing.

Thank you to my family for your support of the goal of doing my part to contribute and make a difference.

Open Stance Postures

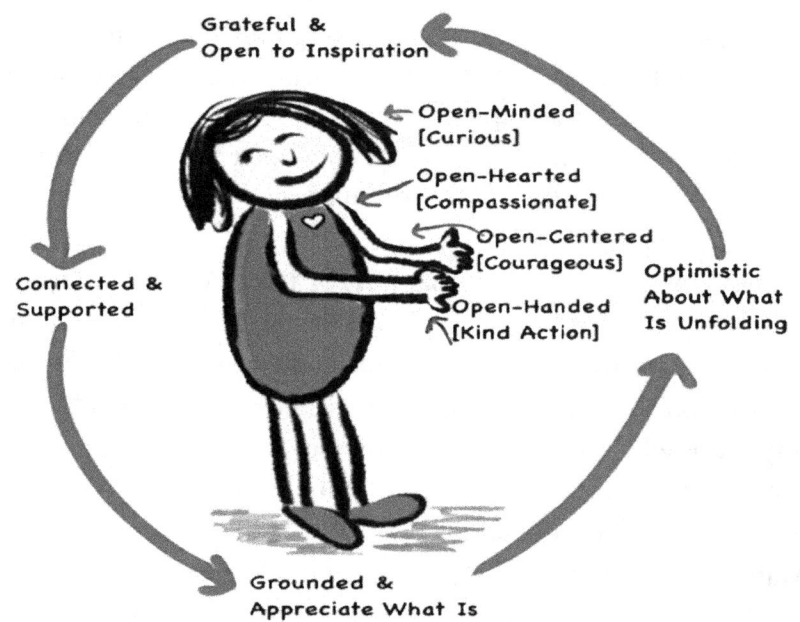

Contents

Introduction 1

Part One
The Case for Being Open 19

Part Two
The Process of Shifting to Being Open 57

Part Three
Practices for Embodying an Open Stance 85

Part Four
Taking Action from an Open Stance 149

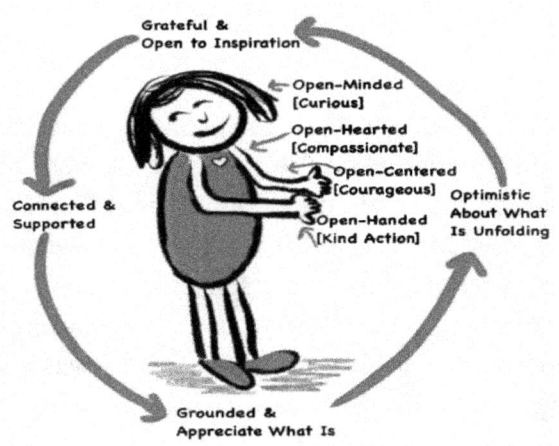

Introduction

"If the first two decades of the twenty-first century have taught us anything, it is that uncertainty is chronic, instability is permanent, disruption is common, and we can neither predict nor govern events. There will be no new normal. There will only be a continuous series of not normal episodes defying prediction and unforeseen by most of us until they happen."

— Jim Collins

MY LAST DAY OF WORK left me tighter than a wound-up clock, my heart clipping along at such a pace that I had little awareness of my surroundings, what I was feeling, or even where I was going! My mind was racing with all I had to do. I was on automatic. Somehow, out of force of habit, I made it to the airport, surrendered into the flight, and let it take me wherever it would.

It would ultimately take me to the island of Santorini, Greece, a place that until then I'd only dreamed about, and several months earlier made arrangements to visit. Ah! This was the oasis I'd been longing for. The blue skies and clear aqua waters with the volcanoes in the distance captured me. I could feel my body slowly unwinding, opening up, and softening with the gentle sea breeze. The unique white buildings with blue rooftops and window boxes with bright fuchsia flowers were enlivening. I felt the warm sun and cool breeze, and my body relaxed. I felt open to drinking in the beauty. I swam and felt refreshed. I appreciated the sound of the herd of donkeys as they ran down a path, and I embraced local artists' creations. I smiled and enjoyed the moment. While I had planned activities, I just wanted to be still and experience this new sense of openness and aliveness. In this state of being open, I felt an expansive possibility about what I could do and who I could be going forward. I was grateful and excited about living.

My heart was opening to this most delicious experience. And my mind was at rest. I felt transformed. I was excited about the possibilities that might emerge and sensed the joy of being open!

Santorini was a once-in-a-lifetime mini-vacation of pure joy for me. Nonetheless, it was a miracle beyond the splendor of that time and place. To be sure, one does not have to travel beyond one's own home to experience such an oasis. The priceless gift I took away was the mindful awareness of what it feels like to be *closed (ungrounded and not present, stressed, judgmental, not connected with self or others)* as distinct from what it feels like to be open *(receptive, aware, empathetic, curious, accepting, anticipating possibilities)*. Within seconds, my physical body felt different. My mental attitude shifted. My heart was at peace. The dramatic shift left an indelible imprint.

While my visit was many years ago, I've "revisited" this experience countless times since then. Knowing I feel better, more awake, and more compatible when I am open, I have been on a mission to recapture what that feeling is about, not only for myself but for my clients, friends, and others. Let me explain.

Being a person who always tries to do too much and puts pressure on myself, I was used to experiencing stress and worry most of the time. Even though I have persisted and been "successful" in life, I certainly did not always experience the joy of being open. Instead, I was judgmental toward myself, others, and situations.

Awareness

One of our greatest challenges is how we work with our thought processes. We have 65,000 to 80,000 thoughts a day, and 95 percent of them are repeats from the day before. We each walk around with whole commentaries on what we are experiencing. We think the voice that narrates our story is correct. Its role is to protect us and keep us safe, and its narration is based on our conditioning—be it from our childhood, education, work, or other experiences. You can bet that in any group, people are having very different experiences based on their perceptions. Of course, our internal thoughts influence our interactions and actions. If we believe someone is not trustworthy, we will guard information. If we believe someone is competent, we are more willing to work with and trust the person.

It is useful to become aware of our thoughts and yet not believe we are our thoughts. We each have an internal spin doctor who tells stories about us, others, and situations. Our spin doctor operates with biases unconsciously and twists perspectives to make us look good and others less so.

One of the most valuable skills we can develop is to be respectful and attentive with curiosity and compassion. The simple action of giving attention to ourselves, others, and our environment opens the door to possibilities. Most of us rarely receive such open and supportive attention. In fact, we pay coaches, therapists, and other professionals for the transformative power of aware listening without judgment.

Today's complexities and uncertainties offer challenges to most people for how to be resilient, experience wellbeing, and thrive. Many feel overwhelmed, and it's becoming clear that traditional ways of managing, parenting, leading, and influencing are no longer adequate to address today's challenges. In our global interdependent world, the scale of challenge is unprecedented. Answers are not readily available, and rather than contract and push for our positions, we will be better served by noticing our internal reactions and shifting to being open to new perspectives, new ideas, and co-created solutions.

In these uncertain times of disruptions, vast technological and collective world changes, polarization, challenges, and trauma, knowing how to be open to *what is* and flexible to respond rather than react to uncertainty is one of the most critical skills needed. When you approach life with an open stance, you can observe more clearly what is present without collapsing into a stress reaction or disassociating and blaming others and/or yourself. You will be better able to choose actions for greater impact and success. When you adopt an open mindset and open stance, you expand possibilities and experience more aliveness and joy.

Backstory

I grew up in a large family with parents who saw the world completely differently. I could see from both of their perspectives so I tried to help them see each other's perspective, but with little success. I encountered the same challenges in the work world, among friends, and just about everywhere I turned. *How can people be productive together when they are literally seeing things so differently?* I wondered. When I was a manager for a Fortune 500 company, it seemed the biggest challenges involved getting people to work together, to trust one another, and to be aligned. Often, the most intelligent people had the most difficult time working together. I knew there must be a way for people to communicate more effectively and to achieve more together.

Affected by what I'd seen at work and in my personal life, I pursued a doctorate in Organization Psychology and studied transformational leadership and executive coaching. I worked with all kinds of organizations to create environments of respect and productivity.

As a global executive/team coach and organization development consultant, I have worked with many leaders, teams, and organizations. Through that process, I have realized the negative impact of polarization, judgment, bias, and stress; all of these keep people closed and not realizing their potential. After working with many teams and organizations to address diversity challenges and create inclusive and engaged cultures, I realized that if people could notice when they became closed to themselves and others and shift to being open, more possibilities and co-created solutions would be available.

After years of developing and facilitating cultural change and diversity and leadership programs and coaching leaders and professionals, I synthesized a process for effectively relating. I created a system based on experience and research identifying what people do well when they are connecting. I identified five essential moves or skills that support positive and productive relationships and emotional and social intelligence. I believe the process of shifting to being open is one of the most critical skills for success in times of change and uncertainty. I wondered how I could assist leaders and team members in finding their oases amid the arid deserts they were creating and experiencing.

OASIS Conversations

The OASIS Conversation process has been successfully tested with managers, leaders, and professionals across the globe for several decades. The OASIS Process works across cultures because it is based upon how humans function. Organizations such as the United Nations, CVS Health, New York-Presbyterian Hospital, GE Capital, World Bank Group, Ford Motor Company, Caterpillar, and Cleveland Clinic have reported benefits from learning and using the OASIS Conversation process. Coaching clients across the globe from Fortune 500 corporations, not-for-profits, and government organizations report significant changes in their workplaces, families, and communities as a result of applying this process. Many who have read the book *OASIS Conversations: Leading with an Open Mindset to Maximize Potential* report positive shifts in their relationships and they experience more ease and confidence in their interactions. Open-minded interactions lead to greater results in all domains. Believe me, if I can learn it and have successful relationships, then anyone can.

The OASIS Conversations course and book focus on how to have positive and productive conversations with others who have different perspectives (everyone). This book and the related Open Stance course are directed toward enhancing our internal conversations and building the mental muscle of shifting from being closed to open. I believe embodying openness is a critical skill for thriving amid differences and uncertainty.

I have devoted my life and career to supporting openness within people, teams, organizations, and communities. I have been fortunate to witness amazing transformations when people shift from reacting to being open and adopting an open stance. I am committed to sharing the process of taking an open stance so people can experience more joy and work together to make teams, organizations, families, and the world better for all. If ever we needed more openness and open-minded conversations in the world, it is now.

Purpose

My goal in this book is to inspire you to commit to adopting an open stance, essentially making the case that being open is the path to resilience, wellbeing, and thriving. To this end, I will provide a process for building the mental fitness of becoming open and practices that will support you in opening to others, yourself, and the greater environment. My wish is that, as a result, you will enjoy life more and will support yourself and others in creating healthier and more productive relationships and environments, thereby making the world a better place for all. My hope is you will often ask yourself, "Are you open?" and notice if you are contracted or in judgment—and then shift to being open. May you find this process enjoyable and revitalizing,

and may you find your own oasis like the one I once experienced in Santorini. In fact, I encourage you to start collecting those moments in your life when you feel open and alive and allow yourself to embody and relive them. You will be able to call on those moments often when you are closed, the way I have often revisited my Santorini *oasis*.

Being Open

What does it mean to "be open" or take an "open stance"? It means being grounded, present, and appreciating *what is*; it means being optimistic about what is unfolding, being grateful, expecting inspiration, and being connected with myself, others, and the environment. In addition, when we are open, we are open-minded/curious, open-hearted/compassionate, and open-centered/courageous. We are ready to take kind action. (See the Open Stance Postures model on the opening page). Being open generally means some combination of being accepting, respectful, approachable, receptive, aware, curious, honest, and willing to listen or try something new. It is a felt experience that we carry in our physical body, generally associated with a feeling of relaxation and aliveness, where we are willing to be influenced and to be flexible to change. When we are open, we are our best selves. We are thoughtful and discerning.

We are each open and closed at different times. It is our nature. When we naturally close, we can be reactive, judgmental, ungrounded and stressed rather than choicefully responsive, present, receptive and anticipating possibilities. We can be defensive and protective when we close. A critical skill is being aware of when we are closed and being able to shift to being open.

Being human, we observe different things and make assumptions and interpretations based on our background conditioning. We have developed habits and routines that serve us in being effective and efficient in our daily lives. For example, we may have a route we take to work each day, which becomes part of our routine. And then the day comes when there's a construction/detour sign, and we've no choice but to go a different way. Depending on how open or closed we're feeling, we may react positively or negatively to the disruption and necessary change. These habitual patterns also cause us to quickly jump to conclusions about "right or wrong." We are quick to believe that things should be a certain way and that our view is "right," and therefore, others' views or situations are "wrong." We quickly become closed to new information or points of view.

Being Closed

We have all had the experience of believing our perception is correct and becoming closed when faced with a different perspective. What is it to be closed? We naturally become closed to protect ourselves, to be safe, and to try to control people and circumstances. We often become closed when faced with the need to change or when encountering opposing views. With awareness, being closed can serve us by giving us space to reflect and determine our next move. Being closed is often associated with having set ideas, intractability, growing wary, being pessimistic, becoming judgmental, and sometimes refusing to listen or make an effort to understand the "other side." For example, we're shocked that someone does not see how our proposal makes so much sense. We are prone to feel negative about the other person and their ideas when they disagree.

When we are closed, we narrow our view and literally [physically] contract. We even hold our breath. Usually, our bodies feel tight and turned inward. When we are in a closed state, we literally cut ourselves off from possibility and promise. It's as if we shut down and close the door to our hearts and minds (not to mention the door to the hearts and minds of others), often without even being aware, conscious, or intentional. It is natural to close, and when we notice our reaction, it allows us to take a closer look at what may be needed. Without awareness, we may react rather than respond.

Of course, today we can find plenty of daily examples of how we react to differences at home, work, and in our communities. We have red and blue states and polarization around gender, sexual identity, social justice, and religious views, among other things. And more often than not, the result is more negative than positive. Unfortunately, this is where negative attribution theory comes into play. We assume negative intent on the part of others with whom we disagree—and as a result, we often become even more entrenched in our own point of view. Some would call this being "stuck in our ways."

We know we have each had various life experiences that influence our perspectives and beliefs. Some of these beliefs are clear to us while others are less conscious. Our bodies have a way of alerting us to danger when our beliefs and self-identity are threatened. We naturally experience tension in the face of a difference; we contract and become closed. This is a natural process that helps us keep our identity and sense of self. Can you imagine if we remained totally open, without this built-in mechanism? We would find it hard to live as we changed so rapidly. However, we can also remain too tightly closed and miss opportunities to grow and experience more and create more.

How do we manage our conditioning and human nature to protect ourselves from being too tightly closed and instead be open to the world around us? We must first recognize our propensity for closing to differences and make the intention to be open to multiple perspectives. We must notice our inclination to feel "right" when faced with a different view. Then we can consciously stop, step back, cool down and shift to being open and curious. We can learn to be open, to embrace more possibilities, and to experience life more fully.

Embodied Awareness

The path to taking an open stance begins with awareness. Too often, we go through life numb to our feelings, preoccupied with everyday frustrations, obsessed with work, overwhelmed with responsibilities, and generally focused on "getting ahead" or some version of what that means. As the pace intensifies and the world order becomes less certain, we lose sight of what's important, particularly how we relate to others and contribute to our spheres of influence.

We can be more aware of our assumptions, emotions, and related "felt sense" in our bodies. With our intention to be more aware and open to multiple perspectives, we are more apt to consider new ways of looking at things, different outcomes, or even the possibility of learning and thriving in the new environment.

An open stance is more than intellectual curiosity; it is an embodiment of a state of mind and being. Our bodies hold the beliefs, values, and emotions that prompt our behaviors, including the trauma of being wrong, out of control, embarrassed, or ashamed. Thus, we must be willing to examine the experiences we're holding in our bodies and how they influence our willingness to be open. Being open is about being emotionally intelligent, aware, and willing to explore new behaviors. Truth be known, more often than not, we are not mindful of feelings and don't even have much of a vocabulary to describe them. We need to get better at recognizing and appreciating our emotions and those of others. Naming our feelings allows us to shift from the amygdala part of our brain, with its cortisone-induced reactions, to activate our brain's neocortex, where we can take in new possibilities and choose more thoughtful, aware responses.

The key skill is to notice when we experience tension and begin to close or contract and to then Stop and Step Back to cool down. This gives us some space from immediately reacting to a different view with aggression or by collapsing or leaving. We can then ensure our safety. Each situation will be different. Sometimes we will need to take a breath and remember that we are okay and have the skills to engage. Other times, we may need to disengage and take a time-out to cool down the cortisol rushing through our body. Sometimes we may need to have a facilitator or outside party to support a conversation. In cases where the threat of violence or physical danger exists, we may choose to fully disengage. There is value in honoring our propensity to close down and seek safety and then to skillfully return to being open.

Once we have Stepped Back and cooled down and feel safe, we can Shift to being open where a different part of our brain is engaged. When we are feeling safe and open, we will hear in a different way and ideally see new connections and understanding. When we attend to our own inner environment and ensure our safety, we are better prepared to attend to the climates we are creating in our interactions.

Yes, it sounds simple, and yet it takes commitment and practice. Being open or adopting an open stance is one of the most essential skills and mental muscles we can develop these days when faced with so much disruption, uncertainty, diversity, and polarization in our global community.

It is easy and natural to become frustrated with the challenges we face. However, when we choose to be open, we can actually enjoy the journey. Through practice, I have learned how to settle myself and to appreciate multiple perspectives. I now notice when I am judgmental (constricted) and can shift into a more expansive open state. As a result, I believe I am a more effective leader, parent, and influencer. No doubt, I am enjoying life more from this open perspective. I believe those around me are also reaping the benefits and are more hopeful. I assure you this open state is doable!

I sometimes wonder if the joy of being open is simply being in the moment with an acceptance of *"what is,"* including the pain, the positive, the mundane, the human experience—trusting life and allowing it to unfold. When we are less resistant and therefore less contracted, we can embrace life, be loving, and receive love. In this state, we are better able to "listen," "to lean in softly with a willingness to be changed by what we hear."[1]

Examples of Shifting from Being Closed to Being Open

---

1. Nepo, Mark. *The Exquisite Risk: Daring to Live an Authentic Life.* New York: Three Rivers Press, 2005.

We all face challenges, disruptions, and trauma. It's part of living. We experience small irritations every day, such as when a colleague or family member disappoints us, or we are simply overlooked rather than recognized. We also face larger collective challenges, such as a pandemic, job uncertainty, financial stress, and climate changes that affect our environment.

How do we react or respond to the large and small disruptions? As humans, we often react by shutting down or by feeling tight, anxious, or overwhelmed. It is easy to collapse into a stress reaction or disassociate and blame others. Our human nature is to react to perceived negative occurrences by fighting, fleeing, freezing, or appeasing. Each of our choices has consequences. What is essential to recognize is there is a choice point, i.e., that point at which you choose to respond with a stance of being present and open to the possible opportunities rather than succumb to the natural tendency to close down, blame, or be self-critical.

More than ever, the skill of responding by being open supports us in being resilient, successful, and thriving. This stance is most critical these days in the face of volatile change, globalization, profound technological changes, and collective world changes. Mind you, being open is not necessarily about being some kind of Pollyanna who only sees the positive. It is noting our emotions and becoming at peace in the present moment without judgment, accepting what is and allowing what will be to unfold, and choosing our actions. The examples below illustrate what it means to shift to being open.

Sarah was excited about the birthday gathering planned for her spouse's big day. A lot of thought went into some special details. Family and friends were attending. When a particular family member walked in, it was abundantly clear they were in a bad mood. Their expression was grim, and their demeanor was gruff. Sarah immediately worried that the event would not be as festive as she had hoped. She was instantly angry at the relative for ruining the atmosphere. Then she paused. She recalled that emotions are contagious and that she could influence the mood of the room. She chose to remain positive and open. She consciously smiled at the relative. She recalled an oasis moment where she was open and remained upbeat. She noticed that the relative and others started becoming calmer within minutes and began joking with her spouse. The event was a success.

Sarah didn't allow herself to get derailed. She knew the power of being open and realized she had a choice regarding how she would respond. She took a deep breath, choosing to be at ease and to positively influence those around her.

Since becoming more aware of my own responses, I've begun to notice the times when I feel open and expansive. For example, I feel open when I am traveling and in different environments. I can remain curious and grateful just to be in a new place. I let myself enjoy challenges, such as getting around an unfamiliar town or ordering food as a vegetarian when I don't know the language. I love photographing sites and nature, taking in what I see with fresh eyes. I can relax my judgment about different things. These very things could be perceived as annoying if I didn't choose otherwise. It's almost like I let myself go and feel present to what is and optimistic about what will emerge next. I trust I will find my way, and I am grateful for all that I encounter. I mostly enjoy working in another country when I can respectfully engage in conversations with others. I find being in this situation enlivening.

In a totally different context, I find I also experience the joy of being open when coaching a leader or a team. Then I am generally fully present, grounded, and alert in my body. Even when a meeting gets off to a rocky start or the endstate is still uncertain, I am generally able to remain optimistic about what may emerge. I believe I bring compassion and empathy to my clients because I appreciate the challenges humans face. And I'm not afraid to share myself and take some risks, creating experiments where they can learn. With years of practice, I've learned that the success of my work with clients fundamentally depends on my being open and creating safe environments.

On a more personal note, practicing yoga, drawing, reading, learning, being with friends and family, and walking in nature are all experiences that give me that same sense of openness and joy of being in the moment. In each of these situations and many others, I notice

I am present, allowing the experience to unfold. I am not contracted or resisting the moment. I have space for what is present and what is emerging. My negative inner chatter is quieted, and I feel alive.

On the other hand, in situations when I am judgmental toward myself and/or others and resistant to what is taking place, I am apt to feel contracted, overwhelmed, and not fully present. I may note I am closed on the continuum of being closed or open. For example, when my partner and I disagree on how we should best approach an issue, or when someone does not satisfy a commitment, I may initially become negative and fail to see many options. I can get stuck in that place of judgment where there is no compromise, only "I'm right; they're wrong." This is a very different experience for me than being open. The negative sensations (tight shoulders, taut mouth, cold hands) and emotions (disturbed, frustrated, aggravated) are uncomfortable cues or signals for me to notice my closed state, recognize what is important, and make other choices. Unfortunately, I sometimes don't immediately notice my closed state when I'm in it and don't feel at choice. This is why I have found it valuable to check in often and ask myself, "Are you open?" When I am more aware, I can recall my intention to be open and shift.

Self-Perception

One challenge with the concept of being open-minded or closed-minded is that most of us believe we are open even when we are not. A friend advised me not to write about being open since most, including her, do not think it applies to them. According to Shane Parrish, in his blog Farnam Street, "Before you smugly slap an open-minded sticker on your chest, consider this: closed-minded people could never consider that they could actually be closed-minded. In fact, their perceived open-mindedness is what is so dangerous." I agree that most of my clients tend to blame others and think that colleagues and staff are closed-minded, and that is the problem that needs to be addressed. Inevitably, they need to make some adjustments. To be an effective leader, we need to start with ourselves.

Brothers Jerry and Sam, leaders of a company, believed they were open-minded. Each owned half of the family business started by their parents more than forty years earlier. While the company had been prospering, the brothers were fighting with one another, and the organization's future was in jeopardy. Jerry believed Sam was too reckless with decisions and spending money. Sam felt Jerry was too conservative and too detail-oriented, and he criticized him for the time he spent on projects and how he managed. When I was brought in to help them communicate, it was clear they saw things differently, and each was being closed to the other. Each owner felt his view and style were right. Neither of them looked inward. Both could only focus on how "wrong" the other was. They were literally each stuck in being "right," leaving them both feeling angry and hopeless.

As an executive coach and organization development consultant, I encounter many situations where people are closed. The consequences can be significant. There appears to be an inherent resistance in our culture to being "wrong." That is, we often feel a strong need to be "right." When we let go of our need to be right and not wrong, we become less authoritative and more curious. We declare fewer opinions and ask more questions. When we are vulnerable and open to learning, we discover new opportunities.

I encounter many leaders who believe they know what is right and are not open. For example, an executive leader was brought into a corporation based on his broad experience. All hoped he would help the company as it faced market challenges. Unfortunately, the new leader was pessimistic, felt he knew what needed to happen, and was dictatorial in his approach. He barely listened to the concerns of staff and set about implementing what he thought was right. While the direction he proposed may, in some cases, have been what was needed, the team shut him out. They felt he was not caring and/or empathetic, so they felt no allegiance to him. The more the staff and the leader seemed to be closed to each other, the more the top boss became less open in his perception of the leader's potential for success. I was called in to support the leader and the team. It took listening to each of them and helping them open to each other's perspective before they could even begin to experience connection and take action together. In this case, the leader was willing to be "wrong" or at least to learn and listen with an open mind and heart to a different way of seeing things. He ultimately was successful in his role.

A large manufacturing company that had merged with a competitor experienced many cliques. Employees shared that they did not feel comfortable in the new combined organization, and engagement scores were relatively low. While the leaders expected the two organizations to merge easily, it took time, intention, and skills for team members to "let down their guard," become open and curious with one another, and invest in powerful conversations to co-create shared solutions. The work helped create a safe space for employees to be open, work through their differences, and arrive at alignment.

Students loudly criticized those with different political views at a college campus, both in person and on social media. The critical environment spurred disruption, more judgment, and a lack of perceived safety to express unique views. Clearly, there is a genuine risk when groups are so entrenched in their ways that it is not safe for disagreement. When there are no established boundaries or ground rules, the lines between right and wrong can become blurred.

Of course, we also see the impact of being closed in our families. A teenaged daughter became estranged from her parents when she felt they did not understand or care about her. She shut them out of her life, and the parents became angry. There was little communication, and all suffered the loss of the family connection. The daughter later regretted that she did not receive the support she needed. And the parents regretted not being open and listening with more empathy.

We all experience being closed to parts of ourselves. We tell ourselves, "You are not good enough; you do not look good enough; you are not smart enough; you are a poor parent, employee, or friend." We need to notice these internal voices when we are closed and learn how to shift from self-defeating reactions to allow more open and curious exploration, acceptance, and healthy choices.

During challenging times such as the coronavirus pandemic, with financial and health concerns that could literally lead to death, we naturally experience a higher level of disruption and uncertainty. At the same time, people are experiencing the impact of long-term structural racism and bias. Add to that significant climate disruption and economic uncertainty, and it is no wonder that many are experiencing trauma. Trauma can be defined as "what happens to a person where there is either too much too soon, too much for too long, or not enough for too long."[2] When experiencing trauma, we naturally close and turn away from a connection to focusing on safety and protection. We narrow our focus, and survival becomes our goal. We have limited options when we are closed to connection, change, and possibilities. However, we can become aware and move toward being open where health, learning, and growth are possible. We can learn new behaviors and shift from our conditioned reactions. For example, we can seek support.

Ideally, we will learn many new things during this time of significant challenges and change. Developmental research on leadership[3] identifies hardship as an integral part of what makes an effective leader or person. Lessons learned from one's personal challenges are essential in forming leadership skills and abilities. While these are challenging times, they can be reframed as opportunities to understand, address our conditioned reactions, become open, and build new habitual patterns to become effective leaders, parents, and influencers. In these difficult times, we can adopt a mindset of seeing challenges as opportunities for development. We can learn how to be more compassionate, take other perspectives, enhance our curiosity, build our courageousness, and increase our flexibility. Hardships can help us to expand our self-awareness, so we are better equipped for future disruptions. Surviving such challenging experiences supports resilience, where we are stronger and more capable of facing future demands. Organizations can also see this disruptive time as an opportunity to create a clear vision, build alignment, and co-create innovative solutions.

This book shares the case for being open in Part One, a process for shifting to being open in Part Two, and practices for embodying an open stance in Part Three. Part Four encourages us to take action

---

2. Duros, P. and D. Crowley. "The body comes to therapy too." *Clinical Social Work J.* 42 (2014): 273. doi:10.1007/s10615-014-0486-1.
3. Center for Creative Leadership: https://www.ccl.org/articles/leading-effectively-articles/3-unexpected-gifts-from-hardship/.

from an open stance to make life better. May you enjoy the process of becoming aware and influencing those around you to create positive and productive environments where you and others realize potential and thrive.

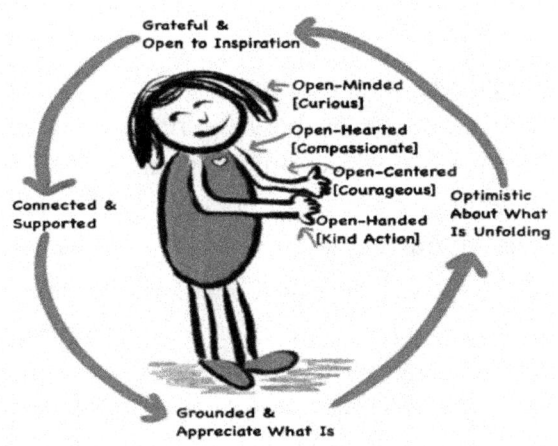

Part One

The Case for Being Open

"As you start to walk on the way, the way appears."
— Rumi

Outcomes of Taking an Open Stance: Resilience, Wellbeing, and Thriving

WHEN WE ARE CLOSED OR contracted, we experience fear and anxiety and our choices and vision are limited. The outcomes of adopting an open stance are resilience, wellbeing, and thriving.

Resilience may best be defined as the ability to recover quickly and a kind of innate toughness that allows one to adapt well to adversity, threats, or other sources of stress. It assumes a kind of agility and flexibility that could be perceived as openness. The practice of being open or resilient is valuable, no matter what we are experiencing. Clearly, life offers many challenges, personally and collectively. The coronavirus pandemic caused health concerns, financial disruption, career changes, and inequities. Even without such a pervasive underlying threat, we each face day-to-day disruptions such as health issues, work concerns, car accidents, property damage, and conflicts with others. No matter how good or careful we may be, life always challenges us with the unexpected. The unforeseen can either knock us off center and off of our game or serve as an opportunity to learn and grow. It all depends on how we react or respond. And the way we respond depends on how much openness and resilience we have worked to develop. The path to openness is a path to resilience, and both are critical to our wellbeing.

Wellbeing may be loosely considered a state of comfort or contentment. At some level, we all strive for wellbeing. It is a felt sense of ease that also aligns with open-mindedness and open-heartedness. When we see ourselves as competent at taking an open stance, we have the confidence that we can respond to what life presents. When we shift from feeling disempowered or victimized, we can embrace an open stance and take comfort in the awareness that we can cope successfully. An internal sense of wellbeing translates to greater health and success. We know this because of neuroplasticity, the brain's ability to make new connections even if we have faced trauma and/or did not have positive role models. Feeling grounded, centered, and at ease is the basis of wellbeing.

Research has identified the importance of wellbeing for the past few decades. While different theoretical perspectives exist, most associate wellbeing with vitality, happiness, involvement, self-awareness, acceptance, congruence, and connection. Many organizations are creating programs and measuring employee wellbeing with the assumption that wellbeing is correlated with individual and organizational performance. Employees are more engaged when they are open and experiencing wellbeing. Greater engagement and wellbeing correlate with greater financial success and a more significant impact.

When we are thriving, it generally means we are flourishing or prospering, regardless of circumstances. In some ways, thriving is a state of being that depends on our individual worldview or values. Nonetheless, thriving is the ultimate state of being open. To me, thriving is where we experience equanimity, being fully alive, and achieving our full potential. We are creative, innovative, and at ease with ourselves. Ideally, when we are thriving, we are our authentic selves—open, honest, and capable. Teams that are thriving are aligned, innovative, and creating significant results.

I hope you can imagine the benefit of catching yourself being closed and reactive; and instead, commit to being open, responsive, and more at choice in your actions.

The Power of Mindset

"There are two ways to live your life. One is as though nothing is a miracle, the other is as though everything is a miracle."

— Albert Einstein

"If we learn to open our hearts, anyone, including the people who drive us crazy, can be our teacher."

— Pema Chodron

Managers and clients often say things like: "Who can you trust these days?" "Watch out for them." "They are wrong." "Things are going downhill everywhere."

Others say: "Look at the bright side of things." "We have a lot to be grateful for." "I am curious about what they are thinking." "I trust things will work out."

Our expectations reflect our deeply held points of view. These points of view form our mindset, a pattern of thinking that we hold about ourselves, others, and the world. Our mindsets are beliefs and attitudes that influence how we interact and behave. Like a fish that may not realize it is in water, our mindsets are often almost invisible to us. They operate in the background and quietly influence the choices we make. It takes conscious reflection to reveal how established and embedded our mindset actually is.

A mindset, such as "the glass is half empty," becomes a filter through which we see and experience daily life; it influences what we see as possible. A mindset actually helps us to simplify the vast amount

of information available. For example, Allie has a pessimistic mindset and, therefore, frequently talks about not being successful. Because she expects things to go wrong and for people to try to take advantage of her, she can appear harsh in her interactions. Her mindset frames her expectations, which then become a self-fulfilling prophecy. Her colleague, with a more optimistic mindset, expects things to work out and people to be kind. She asserts that her expectations are often realized.

Research in recent years is showing that our mindsets are, indeed, potent influences on our experience and outcomes. For example, research on the placebo effect[4] shows that a person's expectations of healing engage areas of the brain that lead to healing outcomes. Simultaneously, research on the "nocebo" effect shows that when a patient expects a treatment to have a negative impact, they are likely to have a negative experience.

Research by Alia Crum[5] at Stanford shows that a person's mindset influences the benefits they derive from behaviors. Subjects in a study experienced reducing the hunger hormone ghrelin when they assumed they were drinking an indulgent calorie-laden milkshake and an increase in the hunger hormone when they drank a "guilt-free lite" milkshake. The satiation levels were influenced by expectations rather than the actual caloric intake, which was the exact same in each situation.

---

4. Crum, A. J. and D. Phillips. "Self-Fulfilling Prophesies, Placebo Effects, and the Social-Psychological Creation of Reality." In R. Scott and S. Kosslyn, eds. *Emerging Trends in the Social and Behavioral Sciences*. Hoboken, NJ: John Wiley and Sons, 2015.
5. Crum, A. J., Corbin, W., Brownell, K. and Salovey, P. (2011). "Mind Over Milkshakes: Mindsets, Not Actual Nutrients, Determine Ghrelin Response." Health Psychology.

Another study by Crum[6] showed that whether people in an organization view stress as positive and supporting focus, or negative and damaging influenced how they experienced stress and their related physiological markers. A study by Langer and associates[7] showed marked changes in the health of people cleaning hotels after a group learned they were actually exercising and enhancing their health on the job. After a short presentation, a simple shift in mindset about the value of their activity on their health even made a significant difference in their physiological outcomes. For example, those who learned they were getting exercise as they worked lost weight, lowered their blood pressure, and were more satisfied.

Research by Carol Dweck[8] at Stanford University indicates that changing your mindset about intelligence and focusing on growth and learning can improve academic and professional success. Other research by Levy[9] suggests that changing your mindset about aging can positively influence your longevity.

Our mindsets are continually being influenced by our media consumption, our interactions, and our experiences. Without awareness of our mindsets, we risk operating based on assumptions and attitudes that do not serve us.

What if we were more intentional and aware of how our mindsets are shaping our lives? What if we saw "challenges" as life opportunities and looked for possible and hidden gifts?

In the face of volatility, turbulence, and diverse perspectives, we want to survive and thrive. Typically, we focus on protecting ourselves and being in control. A mindset is a collection of beliefs we hold about how the world works; it influences our perspective of people, situations, and behavior. Our ideas about the times and ourselves influence how we interact. When we feel threatened, we naturally contract, hold our breath, and make choices for self-protection. Like

---

6. Crum, A., Salovey, P., Achor, S. "Rethinking Stress: The Role of Mindsets in Determining the Stress Response." *Journal of Personality and Social Psychology*. 104.4 (2013): 716-733.
7. Crum, A. J. and E. Langer. (2007). "Mindset Matters: Exercise and the Placebo Effect." *Psychological Science*.
8. Dweck, C. S. *Mindset: The New Psychology of Success*. New York: Ballantine Books, 2007.
9. Levy, B. R. et al. "Longevity Increased by Positive Self-Perceptions of Aging." *Journal of Personality and Social Psychology*. 83 (2002): 261-70.

a horse with blinders, we hunker down, limit our view, and close ourselves off to possibilities. We become critical and judgmental of ourselves and others. We look to blame. It can become a vicious cycle: we grow tired, reduce our options, and make limiting choices.

Our Experience Influences Our Mindset

Mindset: [mahynd-set] noun
1. an attitude, disposition, or mood.
2. an intention or inclination.

— Random House Dictionary

For example, a client grew up in a competitive family; he and his siblings were always fighting for every last cookie! As a result, he thinks it is a "dog-eat-dog" world, where it is necessary to compete continually with coworkers for roles. He goes to great lengths to ensure he emerges on top. He blames and judges those around him when he feels he and his team are not "winning." Ironically, his worldview of competition and seeing others as foes influences those around him, fostering an atmosphere of distrust, discord, and disagreement. As a consequence, he grows more convinced that he needs to compete even more fiercely. His experiences reflect how feelings and behaviors are not only contagious but self-perpetuating.

Our conditioning and past experiences often form our mindsets. It's helpful to remember that our beliefs and habits may have served us well at some point. For example, my client learned to be competitive as a child, as he competed with siblings for attention. This worked for him in his family of origin. Still, his competitive attitude toward his colleagues and team members actually works against him. His team members don't trust him and do not share pertinent information with him or include him in informal interactions where he could see the larger context. By contrast, if we are raised to see the good in people and adopt an attitude of service, we may naturally look for ways to support others and create a collaborative environment in other spheres of life. Our history, family background, and culture influence how we view the world, including the state of our mind and heart. And without self-examination, we unconsciously continue on with behaviors that may no longer serve us.

Given the power of our backgrounds and conditioning, I realize people are often doing the best they can, based on what they have been exposed to and learned. This helps me be a bit more open and curious when interacting with people with different views. Of course, I believe we can all learn and grow.

To achieve real change in organizations or personally, it is critical to develop self-awareness. It is worth developing an understanding of how our attitudes affect how we experience the world for better or for worse. Studies by McKinsey and Company report that organizations that "identify and address pervasive mindsets at the outset are four times more likely to succeed in organizational change efforts than are companies that overlook this stage."[10]

10. Barsh, Joanna and Johanne Lavoie. "Lead at Your Best." *McKinsey Quarterly*. April 2014.

An Open Mindset-Open Stance

Our mindset naturally falls on a continuum between closed-minded and open-minded. Of course, we move along the continuum at different times, depending on various issues. When we become more aware, we realize where, when, and with whom we typically lean toward closed or open.

The state of being open-minded requires the primary intention to be compassionately curious and respectful toward yourself, others, and the situations or environments we face. It begins with the intent to be open to discovery and learning rather than focusing primarily on safety and avoiding pain. The accepting stance creates awareness of possibilities and mobilizes energy for choices.

Open people are grounded and present to *what is*. They appreciate current circumstances and are optimistic about what is likely to unfold. They experience gratefulness and are often open to new ideas and inspiration. They share connections with others and can receive support as well as give support to others. An open stance involves being curious and recognizing they only see a slice of the big picture. They are open to learning more and remain confident that possibilities are emerging. They dare to be vulnerable and take risks and to admit they don't know everything. They welcome diverse and unique perspectives and take respectful actions.

Open-mindedness incorporates what psychologist Carol Dweck[11] calls a growth mindset—an openness to continual learning rather than having a fixed mindset and a desire to maintain current success without making changes. Another element is the ability to be present in the current state. Ellen Langer, a psychologist, has conducted many studies and demonstrated that the simple process of noticing new things enables us to be present, to experience the world with excitement, and to see new opportunities.[12] Often, we are closed, and ironically, we are not there to notice we are not there. When we are open-minded, we seek new ideas and perspectives.

At the heart of an open stance is the belief that value exists in being open to new ideas, different people, and various perspectives; aspiring to compassion and understanding; and conveying this openness through respect, energy, and aliveness. When we have a closed-mindset, we are focused on being right and being seen as such. We believe we know best and we are closed to others' ideas and suggestions. We look for validation of our ideas. We may turn inward, be negative, and close to parts of ourselves.

An open stance incorporates an open heart where we recognize and appreciate our interconnectedness and human nature. Each person has their challenges and sufferings. When we are open, we are warm, kind, non-judgmental, and accepting of others (even when they behave differently). We recognize that each person has strengths and areas for growth and appreciate that people can change, learn, and develop. With an open mindset, we experience gratefulness and see possibilities. We are also open and compassionate toward ourselves.

---

11. Dweck, C. S. *Mindset: The New Psychology of Success.* New York: Ballantine Books, 2007.
12. Langer, E. J. *Mindfulness: 25th Anniversary Edition.* Boston: De Capo Press, 2014.

I recommend you explore your core beliefs since they tend unconsciously to influence your thoughts, behaviors, and ultimately, your results. If you hold on to the desire to remain open and withhold judgment, you will indeed exhibit more open behaviors (listening, exploring, understanding, and reaching co-created agreements). If you stay closed, you are likely to lead by providing answers rather than asking questions and listening. Close-minded people are less likely to attempt to understand different positions, and they are more quick to judge, believe they have the best answers, avoid criticism, and see disagreements as threats; they experience less expansiveness, limited creativity, and fewer possibilities. Researchers at the University of Southern California found that politically closed-minded people literally shut down at a neural level when presented with information from different political views. Those who were more open-minded were able to entertain opinions different from their own.

A manager, Chris, who was closed-minded, was angry at the head of his division, Vin. Chris felt he was more knowledgeable about the business and that the leader "did not get it." Chris shared his dissatisfaction with his colleagues and a hostile environment was created. Chris was unwilling to have his ideas challenged and saw being right as being a winner. He was willing to fight with his boss and peers to demonstrate that his way was best. When I interviewed the team members and Vin, they all expressed frustration. I worked with Chris, the manager, to help him see that his "closed" mindset and anger contributed to the negative situation. The only person he could change was himself. First, he received empathy from me. This, in itself, lessened his defensiveness. He was gradually able to see that Vin, the head of the division, probably felt unheard, judged, and perhaps disrespected. Over time, Chris was able to calm down, become more curious, and become open to learning more. He began to seek out feedback and became more open to learning about his negative influence on the team environment. He grew more willing to have his ideas challenged and listened more openly to find the best solutions. He became more compassionate, realizing that it must be challenging for Vin to have the division's success on his shoulders. His change in demeanor and openness did, indeed, influence Vin.

Later, Vin told me he felt more positive and open to listening to Chris's view. The whole workplace environment started to shift. In fact, the leader, Vin, became open to new ideas from the group. They implemented changes and experienced significant bottom-line success.

It is not always easy to assess whether another person or we ourselves are open-minded or closed-minded. While we know we are sometimes closed, we tend to focus on the times we are open and evaluate ourselves as being open overall. However, when assessing others, we tend to see them as closed-minded based on our perceptions that they "seem" closed. Suppose we judge someone to be closed, like Chris above. In that case, it affects our experience of psychological safety and comfort with the person and how we relate, including our level of open sharing. When we are closed-minded, it negatively influences the culture of the workplace, family, or community. Of course, being open-minded can create a positive and productive environment.

I have personally found the intention to be open and the practice of continually asking myself, "Are you open?" to be transformative. Alternatively, I also ask myself, "Are you closed?" It allows me to have some space to examine my reactions and what I'm feeling in my body. I also ask myself, "Are you in an oasis or an arid desert?" To me, an oasis represents a safe place of relaxation and nurturance. The desert represents a state of contraction and being fearful and closed. I also find it useful to check if I am able to "assume positive intent" of others. If so, this supports me in being curious and open.

We are wired to react to people and situations that we perceive to be threatening. This sensation alerts us to the need to be aware and reflect. We can ask, "Is there real danger here, or am I responding based on past conditioning?" With awareness, we can choose how to engage. While our judgment serves us in being aware, staying in negative judgment takes energy. I believe our highest performance comes when we are in a flow or open state. I also believe we can build the mental muscle to become aware and shift to this open stance.

Benefits of an Open Mindset and Open Stance

"Life is 10% what happens to you and 90% how you react to it."
— Charles R. Swindoll

Vital benefits of an open mindset and open stance are that you will experience more aliveness, more positive emotions, and better health and wellbeing. Operating with an open mindset enhances our experience and success in life. Most importantly, having an open mindset and stance enhances the quality of our relationships and connections with others. We are naturally more attracted to open people than those who seem to know it all and are self-focused. For example, so-called experts may have little patience with others whom they perceive as less knowledgeable, and thus, they may seem inaccessible or closed.

Intentionally or not, they shut people out. Another example we can all relate to is how when we are stressed by deadlines and pressure to get something done, it is harder to be patient and open to others. People sense our stress and lack of tolerance and may shy away and label us closed. On the other hand, when people sense that managers and colleagues are open to new ideas, feedback, and even criticism, they are likely to be more engaged and experience greater satisfaction.

In a project called Aristotle, Google studied many teams to find out the keys to high performance. They discovered the differentiating factor was that people were more engaged and more trusting when they felt psychological safety. This safety resulted from leaders and team members being open to one another, listening to different ideas without judgment. Members of Google's high-performing teams indicated that they felt they could express their views and opinions and take risks without fear of negative repercussions. When a team member feels their ideas are shut down, they don't feel valued, respected, or recognized, and they are hesitant to speak up freely in the future. This hurts the team climate and positive relationships. When most people work in teams with various locations, functions, and differences, trust and openness are critical to creating positive and productive cultures and environments where innovation is possible.

When we are closed-minded, we quickly consider ourselves an expert and easily discount new or different information. History is replete with examples of how well-meaning people did not pay attention or adopt new ways of doing things. Many were slow to validate that the world is round, the value of penicillin, or the importance of washing hands to avoid the spread of illnesses in hospitals. Experts simply felt they knew better, so they discounted different ways and appeared closed-minded. When we are open-minded, we freely admit we don't know what we don't know and can explore new ideas and perspectives. This openness is quite useful for making effective decisions. Researchers suggest we make thousands of decisions a day. These decisions take energy. When we improve the quality of our decision-making, we can make better decisions and experience positive outcomes. If we have an open mindset, we are likely to consider more aspects of a decision and perhaps be open to others' views.

After years of studying successful leaders, Al Pittampalli concluded that the archetype of leaders having "strong convictions" of their views and "staying the course" was outdated. He learned that many of the world's most successful leaders have a willingness to be persuaded—to be open-minded. Many successful leaders build processes where they challenge their thinking and are open to examining new data. They are willing to admit being wrong about an earlier view. In our increasingly complex world, successful leaders see the power of an open mindset and the value of considering emerging evidence to be advantageous.[13]

Besides, people are more inclined to follow open-minded leaders who are willing to be vulnerable and open to change. It is hard to work for a manager who perceives themselves as always right and is not interested in others' views, thus appearing to be closed. When people feel they are listened to, their ideas are valued, and they are included, then their motivation, engagement, and wellbeing soar. This difference is particularly critical since research by Gallup consistently suggests that as many as two-thirds of US employees are not engaged in their jobs.

Children also feel shut down and less engaged when they perceive that their teachers, parents, and caregivers are not open to hearing their perspectives and providing empathy. Rather than saying, "Because I am your parent, that's why….", caregivers can create more positive relationships and respectful environments by being curious, being open to listening, and being open to being influenced.

A sure sign of being an open-minded leader, parent, or influencer is to inquire and genuinely listen to others' views and gain understanding. We should each seek feedback and recognize that creativity and innovative solutions can come from anywhere. We all need to recognize that we don't know what we don't know and could be wrong in order to manage our natural blind spots of assuming we are open when others may perceive we are not. It is also easy for our egos and sense of identity to be tied to being "right." We need to remember that during these times of uncertainty, no one has all the answers. It

---

13. Pittampalli, Al. *Persuadable: How Great Leaders Change Their Minds to Change the World.* New York: Harper Business, 2016.

is useful to recognize our own and others' resistance to change as a natural response. When we appreciate that resistance is natural, and we are open to listening, we can address concerns more readily.

Adopting an Open Mindset

Given the positive benefit of an open mindset, why do people develop a closed mindset? We do so because it is human nature to protect ourselves and want to be seen as having status and being valued. We tend to think that if we have answers and are perceived to be on top, our identity will be secured. Also, we tend to believe we are being efficient. It takes valuable time to gather more information, and we have decisions to be made. Our ego tells us we are "right," and it is comfortable and gratifying to be so. We sense that we have more control when we believe we are "right."

I have worked with thousands of leaders, teams, and coaching clients to adopt more open, positive, and effective views. The work is about seeing how our habitual ways of understanding the world, and the people therein, may be limited and no longer serving us. Whether we're talking about new leadership; management vs. labor; political, social, economic differences; cultural diversity; distinct religious beliefs; or the feuding relationship of two brothers in a family business, the challenge is the same. To successfully move forward in this diverse world, we must be resilient and receptive to change. We must be open to new ideas. We must at least be willing to listen, even if we don't agree, to different ways of understanding. We must make an effort to hear another's point of view. We need to adopt an open mindset to be innovative and successful.

We engage in habitual patterns that may have once served us, but we can make other choices. My clients and I believe our lives and our impact are magnified when we are open. Being open involves being present, curious, compassionate, and optimistic about possibilities. I believe we can learn to adopt an open mindset and that doing so enhances our potential and ability to thrive. When we are "closed," we tend to believe we know what is "right" and are less curious about listening to other perspectives and possibilities. When we are "closed," we literally fail to take in new data and, thus, aren't open to innovation and change.

We all know the feeling of being closed. Often, we first experience tightness in our bodies. It's a kind of dis-ease that has us on alert. The tightness exhibits itself in a sort of rigidity in how we process what's going on. For example, the following coaching clients initially had closed mindsets. They felt they were "right" and were not open to understanding different perspectives and considering new options.

Neal had been a high performer in an analytical role, and his company saw his value. However, he alienated his colleagues by failing to listen to their ideas. Assuming that he knew what was "right," he pushed for his ideas and people did not want to work with him. This hurt his advancement in the organization, as well as his favorability with his team.

Department heads of a Fortune 500 company did not coordinate and complete a critical project. Instead, each head was fighting for more time and resources for their part of the process, and the overall results declined.

Melissa, a sales leader, did not feel confident she could control her success. She was shut down by the fear of failure and blamed her peers for creating too competitive an environment.

After six months in her new role, Julie was frustrated that she was not getting promoted despite her technical skills. She could only focus on the assumption that she was being held back because of her young age. This assumption precluded her willingness to consider any other reasons.

College students refused to listen to a speaker with divergent views and were deprived of expanding their perspective.

Lori, the mother of a teenaged son, chastised him for playing video games while doing homework. She was sure he could not succeed with this behavior. In the meantime, their relationship was at an impasse.

Jill experienced anxiety and often felt depressed. She had a harsh inner critic and was not aware of how to manage her emotions. She felt like a victim of circumstances, berated herself, and tended to blame others.

Each of these people was operating from a closed mindset. They were judgmental. Initially, they were not curious or open to listening to different perspectives or becoming self-aware. To solve their challenges and succeed, they needed to be willing to adapt an open stance and explore other possibilities. They needed to be open to alternative points of view, to influencing others, and to being influenced.

The good news is we can learn to become more open and to adopt an open mindset and open stance. We can begin to recognize when we are contracted or closed. We can learn to notice how we feel and then choose to shift to a more positive and productive state. We can also detect when others are open or closed and support them in regulating to be more open.

In each of the examples I shared, where people were closed and judgmental, they eventually learned their initial reaction was natural and familiar, a kind of self-protected, default response. Without awareness, they readily fell into habitual ways of behaving and thinking. By intending to be open and asking themselves, "Are you open?" they found benefit in shifting to behaviors that were more receptive and non-defensive.

Neal, who assumed he knew best and alienated his colleagues, subsequently realized he could not implement his ideas without inspiring people to join him. He also became aware that the more resistance he detected in others, the more tight and set in his ways he was becoming. After it was pointed out to him how he was actually sabotaging his own goals, he intended to be more open-minded. He listened and engaged in conversations with colleagues and found even better solutions than he had envisioned. He gained support from others and actually enjoyed his work. Within a short while, he was promoted.

Department heads who were fighting and had poor year-end results noticed that energy was wasted as they and their team members competed for resources and engaged in conflict. They had to experience the failure before they could "see" what was happening. Once they shifted to being open and listened to one another, they created a compelling vision, enjoyed the ease of being aligned as a team, and produced innovative results together.

After being coached to adopt a more relaxed and accommodating approach to working with her peers, Melissa, a sales leader, enjoyed the friendly competition among them.

Julie realized her own fear of failure was getting in the way and holding her back at work. She ultimately received several well-deserved promotions.

After reexamining their intention to establish a welcoming community, the college students took a hard look at what was happening. They were committed to creating a safe space that ensured that different perspectives were heard.

Lori learned to shift her focus to what was going well with her teenaged son. She recognized that blaming him for playing video games kept her stuck in a place that did neither of them any good. He eventually graduated, and they maintained a far more positive relationship.

Jill, who experienced anxiety and depression, adopted an open stance and became aware of her reactions. With coaching, she became self-compassionate and learned to connect with more positive emotions, including gratitude and being present. Recalling oasis moments with her family helped restore her confidence. It supported her in shifting to being open and more positive. She gradually experienced more aliveness, and she reported more productive connections with others.

My favorite examples of shifting to being open are parents who report having meaningful conversations with their children and managers who report a whole new view of a staff member, enhanced motivation, and a positive relationship after an open-minded conversation.

In each of the examples above, the shift to a more open stance took commitment and practice. First and foremost, they had to see the benefit of acknowledging what was or was not happening. They had to look [internally] at their assumptions and at what made them closed to different views and to think they were right. They experienced empathy that, in turn, allowed them to feel the emotional pull of being vulnerable and imperfect as they moved toward change. As individuals, they developed an awareness of their typical mindset and heart-set, and how both influenced their everyday behavior. In other words, the transition to an open mindset and taking an open stance required honest reflection and humility.

When we cite the benefits of being open, we must consider individuals' everyday personal experiences within the context of the tumultuous interconnected, rapidly changing global world in which we all live. Our world is moving faster, with old rules no longer serving us. Entire industries and businesses are changing overnight. More people report being stressed, and suicide rates are up. The military coined the term VUCA (volatility, uncertainty, complexity, and ambiguity) to describe the times. With changes in technology, our environment, social systems, and globalization, we are continually confronting diverse views and more significant challenges. To be resilient and thrive in this rapidly changing environment, we must be open to exploring new ideas and engaging in actions together. In the face of uncertainty, it is too easy to become closed. As a result, we are experiencing more polarization, dissatisfaction, and disengagement in families, organizations, communities, and nations.

David Brooks, *New York Times* columnist and news commentator, suggests that the challenges we are seeing today are less related to progressive versus conservative views and more about being open versus being closed. Many sense that old systems are failing people. As a result, they are voting for candidates who claim they will disrupt the current system. Clearly, this is a time of volatility and uncertainty on many levels. An openness beyond self-interest is needed.

At the same time, many studies emphasize that we need social connection. For example, a survey conducted by the health insurer

Cigna found that nearly half of Americans reported feeling alone or isolated despite the widespread use of social media. According to Cigna's chief medical officer, the findings suggest that the problem of disconnection has reached "epidemic" proportions. Dr. Douglas Nemecek stated, "Loneliness has the same impact on mortality as smoking 15 cigarettes a day, making it even more dangerous than obesity."[14] The problem is widespread. The United Kingdom has appointed a "Minister of Loneliness" to address the challenge. When we are open to ourselves and others, we experience better health, get more sleep, and see new possibilities. We are more resilient, agile, resourceful, innovative, and successful.[15]

The simultaneous polarization among individuals and communities and the growing need for connection is a harmful formula at best. All these factors contribute to a society in which the tendency toward isolation and individualism seemingly outweighs the benefits of coming together in collaboration where we welcome and look out for one another. People are fearful. People are uncertain. And when that happens, they are suspicious and they shut down. The choice to be open is more imperative than ever, not only for our individual wellbeing but also for society's long-term wellbeing. Most importantly, it is a choice! There are costs to being closed-minded. For example, we miss the aliveness of being present, are blind to possibilities, experience fear, and even blame others. We lack inspiration and may fail to support ourselves and our communities.

---

14. https://www.multivu.com/players/English/8294451-cigna-us-loneliness-survey/docs/IndexReport_1524069371598-173525450.pdf.
15. Segerstrom, S. C. "Optimism and Immunity: Do Positive Thoughts Always Lead to Positive Effects?" *Brain, Behavior and Immunity.* 19.3 (2005): 195-200.

An Open Heart Is Integral to an Open Stance

Being open is more than a mindset or just related to being available and present to our thoughts. We also need to have a felt sense of opening our hearts of compassion to our emotions and those of others. This open-hearted compassion is essential during times of uncertainty. Naturally, we react to what we perceive as potential danger. Our emotions are signals that we need to pay attention. Then we need to discern if, in fact, we are in danger at that moment and if action is called for. For example, when Sherrie's position was eliminated in her corporation, her first emotions were distress, worry, and anger. All of these emotions were real and needed attention. She knew intellectually that she would be okay since she had saved money and was marketable. Rather than ignoring her feelings or being swallowed up in them, she became open and aware of her emotions and named them. She experienced warmth toward her mix of emotions. This supported her in being more responsive in her actions than just reacting.

As an ideal parent listens to a child when she has an upsetting experience, we can be open to our emotions and be compassionate. We simply need to listen and be attentive and open to our range of emotions. This self-compassion allows us to connect with the parts of ourselves that are experiencing emotion. We become better prepared to extend our compassion to others. We can appreciate that we are each responding to uncertain circumstances based on our conditioning and habitual patterns. It is natural to react, and we can practice turning an open heart to ourselves and others. We can learn and adopt new behaviors that will serve us in these times. To be an effective leader or human being, we need both an open mind and an open heart.

Our brain has different components or neural networks. Our rational brain is associated with our thinking mind. Our emotional brain is associated with our feeling heart. We can learn to recognize what is going on in our hearts and how we feel. Our emotional brain needs to work in tandem with our thinking brain. Fortunately, in recent years, research on emotional intelligence has helped leaders, organizations, and some schools to promote the critical importance of understanding and valuing emotions.

"It is only with the heart that one can see rightly: what is essential is invisible to the eye."

—Antoine de Saint-Exupéry

Every organ in the human body generates an electric current and an electromagnetic field. The heart's electric current is sixty times more powerful than that of other organs in the body and produces an electromagnetic field with a radius of 6-10 feet. This energy affects those around us. When we are at ease and feeling higher frequency emotions, such as compassion, joy, and peace, we tend to influence those around us more positively and create a sense of connection and coherence. When we are in a state of anxiety or distress, others will sense our incoherence and these emotions become contagious. According to HeartMath, coherence allows others to feel connected and at ease, and incoherence creates disruption and anxiety. Our intention to be open to ourselves and others in a non-judgmental way will create a sense of connection and coherence. This connection may be experienced at a conscious or non-aware level. It is valuable to practice connecting with our hearts and having the intention of being open-hearted. We can simply move our attention from our heads and thoughts to our hearts and imagine being open to ourselves, others, and *what is*.

An open-hearted person shows humility and continues to be open to new ideas and others no matter their level in an organization or hierarchy. They generally are confident in who they are and do not see others and their opinions as threats. They are not defensive but open to learning. This creates a positive environment at home or in the workplace.

An open heart is about being compassionate and sincere and about acknowledging the value of emotions. An open-hearted person is typically warm, kind, and welcoming to others and creates real connections. An open mind supports thinking differently (i.e., opening to new thoughts and ideas). An open heart supports feeling differently (i.e., allowing feelings of compassion and empathy for others). Both are interrelated and needed for effective and positive outcomes.

Recognizing our own emotions and those of others is essential to an open stance. We need to accept our emotions and choose to learn from challenges. With our hearts, we can embrace the uniqueness of individuals and appreciate that we are all human beings with our own emotions, thoughts, ideas, fears, and expectations, sharing space on a planet that belongs to all of us equally. Nonetheless, we learn early to be wary of the unfamiliar, with those who come from different lands, with different religions and cultures, and who "see" their beliefs as "true," and with people who have distinct dialects, skin color, values, and backgrounds. And when we fail to cultivate and nurture our emotional intelligence, both individually and collectively, we lose the ability to see what is essential.

Thus, when our mind is closed, we are more likely to be set in our ways of behaving, in our beliefs, and in our general outlook toward others. If our heart is closed, it's unlikely we will be willing to "see" beyond our rational brain and the logic it relies on to define itself.

It is powerful to expand our emotional vocabulary and practice becoming aware of our emotions and naming them. There are many nuanced feelings beyond happiness, fear, and anger. Perhaps we are frightened or in awe. Although these feelings are not located in the physical heart per se, they are connected to the figurative heart we carry within. We can expand this process to sensing others' emotions and offering empathy—even if we do not agree or have the same experience.

Being Aware of Sensations Supports an Open Stance

Why do some people react negatively when someone offers them feedback? Sometimes it's because it makes them feel excluded from the group. Since the earliest days, our brains have been designed to help us survive. They send us messages to avoid dangerous interactions and also nudge us to take actions that will support us in being more resilient so we can experience greater wellbeing and thrive.

Our brain's limbic systems are designed to keep us safe. We tend to assess interactions and experiences as bad/good, dangerous/safe, or approachable/unapproachable. Suppose we encounter something we don't like or something we interpret to be hazardous. In that case, the limbic system supplies adrenaline and cortisol chemicals that prepare us for fight or flight. If the danger seems severe, we may freeze. Some of us have learned to appease others and focus on prioritizing their needs as a form of self-protection.

If there are no apparent threats, the brain doses us with dopamine to motivate us into action to pursue people and situations that may be useful for survival and success.

Our limbic systems create chemical threats and rewards in response to perceived needs. We have some basic hardwired needs. These include safety (security, trust, certainty), belonging (love, respect, feeling welcomed and included), dignity (identity, status, autonomy, and fairness), and growth (achieving potential, learning, and purpose). When we perceive that our basic human needs are not satisfied, we feel threatened, cortisol and adrenaline are released, and we become closed. We experience constriction or contraction in our bodies.

This reaction is why it is useful to become aware of our physical sensations. We can learn to recognize our reactions and to assess our safety level and how our needs are being satisfied. Often, we are not in life-threatening situations, even though our body is telling us there is danger. If we notice our sensations, we are more capable of choosing our response than reacting.

Brain Research Supports Being Open

"An open-minded person sees a life without boundaries, whereas a closed-minded person can only see what is beyond their eyes."

— Kaoru Shinmon

In recent decades, a plethora of research has supported the interconnection between the brain and the body. I was excited to find research that seems to support that when we are in the open mindset, we are actually activating a different part of our brain that allows us to see more broadly and use our neocortex power. When we are in a closed mindset, we are primarily experiencing things through our amygdala. Our neocortex is essentially offline. When we are focused on protection, safety, controlling, and judging, we don't have our full capacity available to see possibilities.

Research by neuroscientists such as Angelika Dimoka[16] that uses fMRI (functional magnetic resonance) supports that two separate brain areas are activated when we are in the judgmental/reactive state and when we are in the open mindset/responsive state. When we feel threatened by a different view of reality, our protective, fear-based neural network, located in the brain's lower area, is activated. Our hearts beat faster, and we tend to experience constriction since we are often holding our breath.

In her book *My Stroke of Insight,* Dr. Jill Taylor,[17] a Harvard-trained neuroanatomist and brain researcher, shares her experience of suffering a stroke. She experienced a complete cessation of anxious mind chatter and stress when a part of her brain became inoperative. She experienced being open and a great sense of peace, compassion, and joy—even while she became paralyzed. She learned that life felt

---

16. Dimoka, A. "What Does the Brain Tell Us About Trust and Distrust? Evidence from a Functional Neuroimaging Study." *MS Quarterly.* 34.2 (June 2010): 373-396.
17. Taylor, J. B. *My Stroke of Insight: A Brain Scientist's Personal Journey.* New York: Viking, 2008.

fundamentally different depending on which part of her brain was active. She eventually gained access to both parts of her brain. We need both to function effectively in our complex society. We can be aware and shift to being open.

It is easy to lose access to our rational prefrontal cortex when we are reactive and closed. The brain's limbic area, which stores memories, exacerbates the experience of a threat as we recall damaging past trauma. Our stress increases, and our cortisol hormone levels rise. We are then more prone to negativity and distrust.

When the prefrontal cortex neural network, located in the higher part of the brain, is activated, we are more relaxed and comfortable with others. We then become more open and experience coherence rather than dissonance. The release of the chemicals oxytocin, serotonin, and dopamine allows us to feel more trusting and confident. With prefrontal cortex activation, we have access to empathy and creativity.

Cooling down enables us to calm our fear-based neural network. Research shows that the human brain has the natural capacity to experience connection and wellbeing. While we are wired to protect ourselves, this instinct is not enough to ensure our survival. We also need cooperation and sharing to help us prosper. When we are open and we engage in behaviors that support others, we are rewarded with a wave of chemicals that create a pleasurable response. Helping others is often a way to experience a sense of openness and aliveness.

We cannot be simultaneously in the open, peaceful oasis state and also closed in the reactive, stressed desert state. The brain's plasticity allows you to build new circuits. The more you forge neural pathways for openness, the more you will have ready access to them and increase your ability to experience creativity and innovation. Neuroscientist Antonio Damasio finds this open stance state of being optimal for collaboration and effective functioning. We are healthy and at our best when we are aware of being open and taking an open stance.

Nervous System Support for Being Open: Polyvagal Theory

Research continues to support the value of noticing our reactions and working to shift from being closed to open. Neuroception is our unaware automatic scanning process. We naturally scan our environment for threats to assess our safety. We respond to perceived danger with a hyper-aroused fight or flight response or with hypo-aroused reactions and freeze or shut down. Our heart rate increases in a hyper-aroused state, and we can experience anxiety, panic, and stress. Our limbic system is reactive. The most primitive part of the brain, the brainstem or reptilian brain, can cause us to shut down or even faint in hypo-arousal.

Steven Porges, a distinguished university scientist and professor of psychiatry at the University of North Carolina discovered a third system. He proposed the Polyvagal theory, which explores the role the autonomic function plays in regulating affective states and social behavior. The tenth cranial vagus nerve is a very long and wandering nerve that winds through the body. It is a social engagement system that is activated when the environment feels safe. In this state, we are open and primed for connection and communication with others. In this ventral vagus state, we can bond, experience ease and connection, and enjoy life in the moment. Some have referred to this as the "tend and befriend" system.[18] Polyvagal theory has shown that prosocial behavior, social communication, and visceral homeostasis that heals the body is not accessed in the closed hypo- or hyper-arousal states. In fact, social engagement, or what I call the open stance or open mindset, is optimal for daily living. When we feel safe and become open and activate the social engagement system, we naturally seek connection with others.

---

18. Taylor, S. et al. "Biobehavioral Responses to Stress in Females: TendandBefriend, Not FightorFlight." *Psychological Review*. 107.3 (2000): 411–429.

The introduction of Polyvagal theory has helped us understand that much of our suffering and struggles are related to the state of our nervous system. While it is natural to close or contract to protect from potential danger, that system causes us to feel stressed, overwhelmed, worried, reactive, and shut down. However, our survival responses are getting triggered even when we are often not in life-threatening danger. By paying attention and setting an intention to be open, we can learn to shift to being open, activate our social engagement system, and experience more connection and possibility. This is a significant finding that has led to the development of practices that support people in becoming aware when they are stressed or closed and shifting into the tend and befriend or what I call an open stance.

Emotions Are Contagious

Emotions are contagious.

Research has also demonstrated that emotions are contagious. Within milliseconds, our bodies are picking up others' emotions. Elaine Hatfield and colleagues, authors of *Emotional Contagion*,[19] identify the strong influence of positive and negative emotions on others. When we sense that someone is open or closed, we tend to react similarly. Your openness or closed-mindedness can spread to others

---
19. Hatfield, E., Cacioppo, J.T. and Rapso, R. I. *Emotional Contagion*. Cambridge, Gr. Brit.: Cambridge UP, 1994.

and influence the climate. You may have experienced the contagious nature of emotions at a gathering of people. If you walk into a room where people are in conflict, you will likely sense a heaviness. On the other hand, if you walk into a space where people are in a positive mood and enjoying each other, you are likely to feel more upbeat and light. We pick up the emotions of others in a matter of milliseconds, and it can be unconscious.

When judging, we experience the classic fight, flight, freeze, or appease adrenaline reaction to a perceived threat. Our older brain structure and limbic system, which are the human brain's emotional parts, immediately react to potential danger. This happens even before the neocortex, the brain's thinking section, can register the perceived threat and provide rational input. Our reaction occurs so quickly that it appears automatic, so we may not be immediately aware of it. That's why it is useful to get to know our predominant sensation signals and understand when we are closed to new information.

On a physical level, the brainstem reacts to potential danger where rapid mobilization of energy is needed. The brainstem reacts to ensure our survival in the face of a potential threat, an attack, or a harmful event. This reaction served humans well when sensing danger was a literal matter of life and death. Walter Bradford Cannon observed that animals react to perceived threats with a sympathetic nervous system discharge, which primes the animal for a stress response. Humans also respond, and the adrenal medulla produces hormones that affect the response. In a perceived effort to control a situation, some people naturally react in a fight mode and may yell or get angry. Others react more predominantly in a flight manner with fear, which may involve leaving the scene. The freeze response involves pausing like a deer in headlights, almost waiting for the danger to pass. Others may react by actually moving forward to appease others, to address issues, or take care of others as a learned response for safety. We are wired with these essential survival reactions. While we are likely to experience each of these, it is common to have one type of reaction that dominates our patterns. The limbic part of the brain creates emotions that guide us to move toward or away from something.

When we become aware, the brain's cortex allows us to think about a situation and essentially supersede the limbic reaction. We can calm down amygdala-based fear reactions by secreting a neurotransmitter called GABA (gamma-aminobutyric acid) that inhibits subcortical firing. We can then experience more balance and a greater sense of ease. The secretion of the hormone oxytocin, sometimes known as the "cuddle hormone," creates feelings of wellbeing (as does a mother's hug to babies).

When we are experiencing the basic survival response of fight, flight, freeze, or appease, we respond automatically and reactively. We can catch ourselves in this emergency response and shift to an open, receptive state when we are not actually in danger. Most often, we are not in physical danger. We can connect with our natural state of wellbeing and allow our neocortex to engage.

When we can stop and step back from a judgment, we use the power of the middle prefrontal region of the brain to put some space between input and our reaction. This ability to pause before taking action is a critical component of emotional and social intelligence. We can then become mindful of what is happening, refrain from reacting, and manage our impulses as we consider our options and feel more at choice about how we will respond.

The good news is research verifies our brain's neuroplasticity. This means how we focus our attention shapes our brain's actual structure. The more we focus on shifting from judgment or being closed and constricted to becoming open and expansive, the more we shape our brains to be more resilient and experience wellbeing and thriving. Research supports that with resiliency you will not only experience more positive interactions but better overall health. You can actually be enhancing your health and sense of wellbeing as you focus on being more open to different perspectives and different people. We have many opportunities to practice this skill as we interact with myriad people and situations. You don't have to sit and meditate. However, doing so will also support your ability to shift more quickly into a state of openness and non-judgment.

To be genuinely open-minded toward others, we first need to take a supportive and compassionate stance toward ourselves. We all have critical internal voices, so we also need to learn to be open and empathetic toward these parts of ourselves. Our critical voices were formed to serve us and help us survive and manage in our environments. As we mature, these critical voices may not be serving us anymore. By appreciating how they have served us and giving them empathy, we may be able to shift our relationships with them. Research reviewed by Tom Stone[20] shows we have a much greater capacity to process our feelings as we mature into adults. We will develop more than seven times as many brain spindle cells as we had as infants. (Spindle cells are activated with increased blood flow in experiments where subjects are given emotional stimuli. They help us grow our ability to process a broader range of emotions, be more self-aware, and better manage our emotions.)

Resonance

Adopting an open mindset and open stance may also be useful for our individual and collective health. Limbic resonance refers to the energetic exchange between people who are interacting in a caring and safe relationship. The positive interaction stimulates the release of neurochemicals in the brain's limbic region, essential for emotional and physical wellbeing. Without enough limbic resonance in our lives, we function less effectively.

This is why social isolation is unhealthy. We need each other. We mainly thrive when we experience a real connection and a safe and productive environment.

---

20. Stone, T. *Pure Awareness*. Carlsbad, CA: Great Life Technologies, 2007.

Research shows that newborns may die if they don't experience human connection. We are not self-contained, self-regulating units. When individuals interact, their minds become fused into a single system—a neural circuitry. Our systems synchronize with one another and influence each other. We need each other. An ideal parent initially supports a child to co-regulate. As adults, we can support each other in healthy interactions to regulate our systems to feel comfortable to explore, learn, and thrive. When we are open, we open our hearts to empathetically connect with others. This enables us to be more positive and trust possibilities.

In her book *Resonate*,[21] Ginny Whitelaw makes the case that how we resonate or become on the same wavelength with others is a physical fact based on the principles of physics. She suggests that we can become aware of and cultivate how we resonate with others to influence change. We can choose to take an open stance.

In their book *Resonant Leadership*, Annie McKee and Richard E. Boyatzis emphasize a leader's power to inspire or project their wavelength, which resonates throughout an organization or community to unite people and align them for a common goal. We each can be a leader today, whether or not we are in a formal leadership role. By being open and emotionally intelligent, we can support and inspire others to do the same. Through open-minded conversations, people can align around shared visions to make their families, organizations, communities, and the world better.

Boyatzis and colleagues at Case Western University talk about positive and negative emotional attractors or PEA and NEA for short.[22] Each of these states comprises distinct emotional, psychological, physiological, and neurological characteristics that create a force around your thinking, feeling, and behaviors. Based on complexity theory, each state has distinct positive and negative emotional arousal, distinct hormonal arousal, activation of the parasympathetic and sympathetic nervous systems, and activation of different neural

---

21. Whitelaw, G. *Resonate: Zen and the Way of Making a Difference.* San Francisco, CA: Koehler Books, 2020.
22. coursera.org/lecture/emotional-intelligence-leadership/watch-studies-and-neurological-evidence-of-coaching-to-the-pea-o525F

networks. This research supports the difference between the closed and open states we have been talking about.

Barbara Frederickson,[23] a respected researcher in the field of positive psychology, emphasizes that positive emotions such as hope, gratitude, inspiration, and interest are accompanied by a "felt sense" and activation of the parasympathetic nervous system and the neuro network, called the default network. Over time, positive emotions contribute to enhanced health benefits, resilience, and wellbeing. Focusing on taking an open stance is good for our health.

Studies show that being in a PEA state or an open stance leads to increased cognitive and emotional openness and physical vitality. The NEA is related to negative emotions such as anxiety, fear, and despair. When the sympathetic system is aroused, we experience stress in the closed state. We can experience this negative stress by just anticipating danger. The task-positive network in the brain is activated in this state by focusing attention and decision making. Clearly, this network has its benefits. It is useful at times to narrow our focus and close ourselves off to additional data. However, overuse of negative emotions and too much closing can deplete us of energy and cognitive ability. For a sustained change, more PEA or openness is required rather than NEA or closedness. Research suggests the necessity of three to six positive emotions to counterbalance each negative experience to enhance cognitive capacity, a sense of purpose, engagement, and wellbeing. Our families, workplaces, and communities would be healthier and more effective if we spent more time being open or in the PEA. However, 80 percent of us experience negative emotions or being closed more often. The pull of negative emotions and stress is more potent than positive emotions. We all seem to be experiencing too much stress these days. In summary, we need the NEA to survive and protect ourselves, and we need the PEA for being open to thrive.

Tony Jack, at Case Western Reserve University, identifies through various studies that the analytical or task-positive neural network that helps us with working memory, mathematical problems, abstract reasoning, and analytical work has little overlap with the empathetic

---

23. Fredrickson, B. *Love 2.0: Finding Happiness and Health in Moments of Connection.* New York: Hudson Street Press, 2013.

The Case for Being Open / 53

or default mode network that enables us to be open to new ideas, scan the environment, be sensitive to other people, and open to moral reasoning. These two networks are "antagonistic"; they have little overlap and suppress each other.[24] If the analytic network lights up, the person's empathetic network gets suppressed in that moment—and vice versa. We need both of these networks and need to toggle back and forth.

All of this research supports that different parts of the brain and nervous system and different hormones are activated when we are open or closed. While we need to be closed at times for survival, there is a cost to our health and wellbeing of not being open to possibilities.

We Can Change and Grow

---

24. Boyatzis, R. E. and A. I. Jack. "The Neuroscience of Coaching." *Consulting Psychology Journal.* 70.1 (2018): 11-27.

Of course, it is natural to react and become closed to parts of ourselves and others. We naturally seek safety and protection. We react to uncertainty when we don't feel in control. We all experience stress and negativity bias, and we are naturally attuned to unpleasant news and stimuli. We quickly blame and become judgmental.

It is not so easy to make the shift from a reaction such as judgment and protection to being open and non-judgmental with the intention to learn—especially when we have what has been called an amygdala hijack where we lose our cool and react. Perhaps we feel betrayed again and immediately accuse our partner or colleague, then leave the scene before we even realize we are reacting. It happens to all of us. We may be under pressure with a looming deadline and be short on sleep and energy. We all have such reactions that are wired into our survival systems. Common reactions include fight-flight-freeze and appease. Some naturally leave the scene when their amygdala (the emotional center of the brain) is activated. Others stay and fight, and some freeze, like a deer in the headlights, and are immobilized to take the next step. A person who appeases moves toward the other and tries to support and please the other person, often giving up their own needs. None of these reactions is satisfying over time. Yet, we can recover from our reactions. After the adrenaline moves through our system, we can see new options. With practice, we can ask ourselves: "Am I open?" and catch ourselves and shift to being open and curious before we react in ways we may regret.

Researchers used to believe we had little chance of changing as we grew older. However, in the past thirty years, we now recognize our brains' neuroplasticity and the capability to build new responses and habits. This is excellent news. We need to be able to be responsive to our rapidly changing world and to manage our reactions. We can, indeed, learn the habit of being open with intention and practice. We can build the awareness and muscle of shifting to being open. We can practice assuming positive intent and testing our assumptions.

Richard J. Davidson, founder and director of the Center for Investigating Healthy Minds at the University of Wisconsin, Madison, believes the brain is shaped by experience. He says, "I envision a day when mental exercise will be as much a part of our daily lives as physical exercise and personal hygiene."[25] We can build our mental muscle and shape our brain by the experiences we choose. Ideally, we engage in experiences that support resilience, wellbeing, and thriving.

Clearly, we can set our intention to become aware when we are closed and shift to being open. Part One has shown we can practice taking an open stance toward ourselves, others, and our community. Part Two will share a process for shifting to being open and a process for building the mental muscle of being open and creating mental fitness.

---

25. www.centerhealthyminds.org.

Part Two

The Process of Shifting to Being Open

"A bend in the road is not the end of the road...unless you fail to make the turn."

— Helen Keller

A LEADER ASSUMED A MEMBER OF his staff was not a team player and was lazy. The team member was not updating his boss on the status of projects. The frustrated leader talked about letting his staff member go. However, he noticed his judgment signal, which was tightness in his chest and negative self-talk about the staff member. He remembered to Stop before reacting. He was able to Step Back and Cool Down by getting empathy from a colleague. The empathy, where the peer recognized his frustration, calmed him down. He recalled his intention of being an empathetic leader who listened, which allowed him to Shift to Being Open. After his conversation with his staff member, he reported that his view had totally changed. In fact, the person had been actively helping the other team members and was successfully completing his projects. In the conversation, the leader learned that the team member did not realize he was expected to be sharing his progress. He felt confident and did not want to bother his manager. This leader was glad he had noticed his judgment and blind-spot, cooled down, and engaged in a positive and productive conversation. The leader could see he had not clarified his expectations, and he realized he had unfairly written off a productive staff member. He was grateful he had learned the skills for such a conversation, and he approached the team member with an open mind. This conversation supported the whole team.

We can each build the habit and the neural pathways for shifting to being open. We can develop the mental muscle and mental fitness to notice our judgments, refrain from reacting, and be more at choice. Here is a process that has worked for my clients and me. The process can take less than a minute or be spread out over time, depending on the situation. While it is simple, it is not always easy. However, it gets easier with practice.

1. **Stop**. Sense: "Are you open?" Notice your signals.
2. **Step back** and cool down.
3. **Shift** to being open.

The Process of Shifting to Being Open / 59

Set Your Intention to Being Open

"If you change the way you look at things, the things you look at change."
—Wayne Dyer

I hope I have built the case for the power of setting your intention to being open. When we build the mental muscle of shifting to being open, we experience more resilience and wellbeing and we thrive. While it is our nature to contract and seek safety, you can make it your choice to become aware and choose to be open, acknowledge your thoughts and emotions, and decide to learn and be optimistic about possibilities. You commit to being aware and to learning rather than focusing on safety, control, judgment, and contraction. With this path, you will acknowledge the pains of life and seek possibilities. You will limit your resistance to change.

This process is about an intention to be more adaptable and less rigid in mind and heart. I don't think the value of an open stance, which includes an open mind and heart, can be overstated. Many conflicts, disruptions, and challenges in our world evolve from misunderstandings, different perceptions, and a failure to communicate effectively. Our intent affects the way we think, feel, and behave. It is a creative force. When we make an intention, it is the same as setting a purpose or aim. Our intention is our plan for how we want to be. To set an intention of taking an open stance means we are taking responsibility for our inner state and making a commitment to shift to learning even in the face of challenges, uncomfortable feelings, different views, and perceived obstacles. We commit to being kind and compassionate with ourselves and others when we choose an open stance. We are open to noticing our habitual patterns and stepping away from wanting certainty and avoiding change. We commit to refraining from blaming others and circumstances, and we commit to taking responsibility for our feelings and actions. In essence, we are committing to experiencing life from our higher or wiser self. That is, from a perspective that is broader and more encompassing than the context of our own individual needs and wants. When we make a commitment, the path forward often becomes clear.

Make it your plan to notice your current state and shift to being open when you catch yourself contracting and reacting to protect yourself. Research suggests that doing small things often, such as reminding yourself of your intention, will help build the habit and create neural pathways.

We can remind ourselves in many ways of our intention to be open. We can write our commitment on notes around our home. We can state our affirmation when we awake, or we can make it a habit to express our commitment at various points in the day, such as when we enter work or have a meal. We can share our aspirations with trusted others and share our progress too. We can reflect on our commitment by journaling or sharing with others in a workshop.

One way I affirm my commitment each day is to envision the various aspects of being open that are reflected on the Open Stance Postures model (see opening page and Part Three). I reflect on each component of an open stance, including my senses and related emotions. For example, I literally feel my feet on the ground and become centered before entering a meeting. I look forward to the meeting and sense that it will unfold positively. I sense above my head and feel how grateful I am to be working with my client organization. I expect to be inspired and creative. I envision my back and know I have support behind me with warm connections. I reflect on the relationships in my life that support me. I touch my head and confirm I am open-minded and curious about how things will develop. I put my hand on my heart and am compassionate toward my client, what they are experiencing, and myself. My attention moves toward my center. I feel the courage to take risks in the meeting and be vulnerable in sharing myself and my reactions and insights. Finally, I open my hands and physically welcome whatever emerges and all of life. I envision taking kind actions for all involved. I confirm I am open and ready to experience an oasis and be my best self. Sensing each of these aspects of an open stance enables me to embody who I want to be.

Going through this ritual only takes a few minutes. I feel present, open, and joyful as I start my meeting and project. I have made this a part of my daily routine. It has supported me in being more aware and sustained me on the path of embodying an open stance. The key is to experience and embody each of the components rather than just recite the words.

1. **Stop. Sense: "Are you open?" Notice your signals.**

Self-awareness is a crucial skill for being an effective leader, high performer, parent, or influencer, and it is the cornerstone of emotional intelligence. Being attuned to what is going on in our body is often overlooked as a critical component of self-awareness. Typically, we might initially get caught up in our thoughts and begin to rationalize why "I'm right; you're wrong," or be self-judgmental. Or we focus on blaming the "other" for whatever position they might take that is in disagreement with our own point of view. We may also react negatively to circumstances that we think "should" be different. We also numb ourselves with multiple diversions.

When we ask ourselves "Are you open?" or "Are you closed?", it is important that we look beyond our thinking mind and begin with an assessment of what we feel in our body. With practice, you will start to check, and when you notice constriction in your body, you can move to stepping back and cooling down. If you are at ease and open, congratulate yourself and proceed with your activity.

Typically when we are stressed or ill at ease (i.e., closed), we can feel a tightness in some place in our body. It might be in the pit of our stomach or our shoulders or the area in our neck where we swallow. Wherever it is, it is our first clue to whether we are open or closed. Part of the process is becoming aware of where you carry stress. Sense your emotions and name what you are feeling. For example, "Something in me is...angry, happy, sad, concerned, confused, or worried."

Try an experiment. Notice how you are feeling. Perhaps you say, "I feel sad." Now reframe this and use the statement, "Something in me is sad." Notice the difference in your experience using the second statement. Perhaps you feel a bit more space, and in this case, you are not swallowed up in your emotion but are a compassionate observer. I learned this process from Ann Cornell Weiss,[26] who shares a focusing technique based on Eugene Gendlin's work. The latter statement allows you to become aware of your emotion(s) without allowing it to define you.

You will find it helpful to expand your emotional vocabulary. Too many of us rely on basic emotions such as happy, sad, or angry. However,

---

26. Weiss, A. C. *The Power of Focusing: A Practical Guide to Self-Healing.* New York, NY: New Harbinger Publications, 1996.

The Process of Shifting to Being Open / 63

these emotions have many gradients, such as frustrated, irritated, frightened, stunned, fuming, and annoyed. Research has shown that when we name our emotions, we calm our amygdala, and another part of the brain is activated that provides us with a greater capacity to see possibilities. Becoming aware of our emotions and related thoughts or assumptions is the key to being emotionally intelligent. There are apps available now that support you in naming your emotions. The larger our palette in describing our emotions, the more agile we become in responding to challenges.

As a song has music and words, we have thoughts accompanying our emotions. Again, it is a valuable skill to notice our thoughts and assumptions and recognize how they influence us.

Ideally, we can welcome and appreciate all of our thoughts and emotions, seeing them as messengers that confirm what is important. For example, you may be upset about not being included in a meeting because [in your mind] being included means you are valued for your contribution. Noticing what happens in our body when we're excluded, what emotions we're feeling, and what thoughts or assumptions we rely on to make sense of the exclusion are all clues to our awareness. The best thing we can do to avoid getting "stuck" in such an experience is to be compassionate to ourselves and our related thoughts and emotions.

We react to external circumstances as well as our internal thoughts. Using the same example of not being invited to a meeting, we are likely to react. You may assume your colleagues left you out on purpose and something in you feels frustrated. This situation may have happened to you before. If you are unaware of your emotions and thoughts, you could react and say something you may regret later. However, when you notice your emotions and thoughts, you are better positioned to respond with choice. You may engage in conversation with your colleague to find out what happened. If you are open and curious, you may discover the meeting did not apply to you, that you did receive an invitation, that you did not catch notice of it in your emails, or that they were planning a surprise party for you.

An excellent habit for us to develop is an internal check-in to become aware of our sensations, thoughts, and emotions and how our background could contribute to our interpretation of a situation. Perhaps a history of being left out could make us quite sensitive to the issue. At the same time, a friend has an entirely different reaction based on their upbringing and history.

Being self-aware is the defining characteristic of effective leaders and the hallmark of emotional intelligence. Thus, our desire to become aware of bodily sensations, and the emotions and thoughts that accompany them, becomes the most critical step in the process of assessing if we are open. When we can be with and accept our thoughts and emotions with compassionate curiosity, we can learn and respond with awareness. We all long to have a safe space to express ourselves in a non-judgmental environment. Before we do anything else, we must create that space within ourselves.

Notably, when we create a safe space within ourselves that is non-judgmental, we allow ourselves the benefit of a free and open assessment of what is taking place. It is challenging to be open to others, ideas, or differences until we are open to ourselves. So, we have to begin at home. This means we allow ourselves time to reflect, explore, and dig into our background and experience to become clear about why we feel what we feel and how we came to be how we are. And in the long run, we learn how we can let go of some of the beliefs that no longer serve us and be open to a different future.

When we are noticing our assumptions, we can often identify several possible explanations. In our example of not being included in a meeting, we can surmise several possible reasons: a new person sending out the invite and misspelling our name, a problem with our email, an oversight, etc. These are all plausible solutions, and we are open to discovering more.

However, sometimes you notice you feel strongly and you're confident you know why you were omitted: your colleague wants all the credit and did not want you there. You can see no other explanation, and you know you are "right." You sense you have made an accurate judgment. You are not open to other explanations at that moment. You are closed. You may notice a tightness in your chest or stomach or feel the heat in your face. You may hear an inner voice blaming and stating that others are wrong. I believe we each have predominant signals that can cue us in that we are closed. It could be a pain in your neck or shoulders or that your ears feel hot. Our body signals can serve as a cue to pay attention when we are closed.

Why do I suggest you become aware of your body sensations? Our body reacts before we have time to realize we are closed. Have you ever had the experience of jumping out of the way of a bus on a busy street and then saying, "Wow, I could have been killed!"? A signal went quickly to your body to jump before you rationally became aware of the approaching bus. Neuroscience research shows a quick path that leads to our reactions and a slower neural pathway to identify the situation. We benefit by becoming aware of our predominant signals of danger that support us in closing. When I speak about these signals with groups, many are not initially aware of their signals. However, with a little investigation, it soon becomes apparent that we may have several predominant signals. Knowing these signals allows you to catch yourself and hold back from reacting. I have seen a wide range of signals from a tight stomach, shoulders, or chest to a constricted throat and a quick heartbeat.

We need to appreciate that it is normal to react and that we are probably doing the best we can at that moment. Then we can cool down and become open. Or, in some cases, we may consciously choose to stay closed.

How do we survive when our natural bent is to be stressed, biased, judging, closed, and controlling? We recognize our humanity and work on being open first to ourselves and then others. We need to be compassionate about what we are experiencing within ourselves and what we and others face in our turbulent world. While it feels "right" or good to be "right" and push to have things under control, we must learn to be empathetic, curious, and open to other perspectives. This openness is not effortless but well worth the commitment because many possibilities become available when open.

When we naturally contract, hold our breath, focus on safety, and believe only we are right, that natural flow of energy, ideas, and possibilities is contained. Like a dam blocking a waterway, we see and experience fewer possibilities. In fact, when we are judgmental, anxious, and stressed, a different part of our brain is activated. We cannot access the part that is creative, in the flow, and sees many opportunities.

It is worthwhile to become familiar with your predominant signals when you are closed and in judgment. Suppose you pay attention to your interactions and how you feel when you disagree with someone. In that case, you will begin to notice you often experience a flushed face or tight jaw, or a constriction in your throat or chest. I believe that noticing our physiological response is the most efficient way of detecting when we are judging or closed.

When are we closed? We are closed when we are not grounded or centered and do not appreciate *what is*; when we are negative and not optimistic about what is unfolding; when we are ungrateful and feel unconnected and unsupported. We are closed when we are not open-minded or curious, when we are closed-hearted and not compassionate, when we resist taking risks and being vulnerable, and when we feel unkind and disrespectful. Each of these is the opposite of the Open Stance Postures. Of course, we can be anywhere on a continuum for each. We can be closed-minded and not curious about another's perception. We can also be extraordinarily judgmental and be certain the other is wrong.

We each may have a propensity for closing in one of the areas. For example, you may approach life as a pessimist and expect things to go wrong, or you may not appreciate the connections or support around you. We each have had life experiences that have conditioned us to see and experience life differently. Depending on the level of severity, these can be called traumas. I trust that life is a journey, and we can grow and develop through these. Sometimes help from therapists, coaches, and other resources are valuable. I encourage you to seek support if needed. Often, we can change our internal dialogue when we recognize one of our habitual patterns. You may begin saying to yourself, "I recognize and appreciate the connections and support in my life" or "I am recognizing and appreciating all that is going well each day." I will suggest additional practices in Part Three.

In summary, stop and assess. If you notice you are indeed open, acknowledge this and appreciate the stance. However, if you feel constricted and closed, catch yourself before you react by taking a breath and accepting yourself. Recognize that it is human to contract when facing disruption or judgment. Then it is important to step back and cool down.

2. Step Back and Cool Down.

"Between stimulus and response there is a space. In that space is our power to choose our response. In our response lies our growth and our freedom."

— attributed to Viktor Frankl

When we are triggered and may be stressed or defensive, we naturally mobilize to defend ourselves or retreat. At the same time, we lose our full capacity to use our prefrontal cortex and our rational thinking process.

One thing you can do rather than react when you notice you are closed is to take a deep breath in through your nose and count to three. Then breathe out through your mouth as if you are blowing through a straw as you count to six to yourself. This process will force your system to cool down and allow your body and mind to come into equilibrium as cortisone clears in your bloodstream. You may require several of these deep breaths to support you in stepping back and cooling down. It is also useful to put your attention on your body and notice your feet on the ground or your seat on the chair. You may simply put your attention on sounds that are nearby and distant or press your hands together and notice the sensation. Such actions will support you in being more present.

With the intention of being more open, we can develop the skill of catching ourselves when we are contracted, when we believe we are "right" or others and situations are wrong, or when we are experiencing self-judgment and tension. Once we catch ourselves, we are more positioned to cool down. The more we practice catching ourselves and cooling down, the more adept we become at shifting to being open. I say to myself, "I don't know what I don't know," to remind myself that I cannot see everything—even when a part of me strongly senses that I am "right" or I feel stressed and contracted. I remind myself that people are often doing what makes sense to them based on their backgrounds and conditioning. It is human nature to judge ourselves, others, and situations, but we can learn to be open.

Because we are so quick to judge, it is best to notice judgment by our signals. Some notice their voices get louder or quieter. People hold their breath; their heart beats faster; they become pale or flush; they shake their foot or hand, etc. We all seem to have an inner voice that is blaming us or others. Some of these voices are quite harsh.

The Process of Shifting to Being Open / 69

When we notice our signal, we can use it to build the muscle that stops us from yelling, leaving, or reacting, and instead, catch ourselves. At this point, I genuinely feel I am right and want someone to agree with me. Over time, I have learned that at such times I need to Step Back and Cool Down. It is not easy, but through practice, we can become more effective in this process and refrain from reacting.

Developing your own strategies for cooling down and experiencing an open stance is also vital. Examine your assumptions and beliefs to discover how likely they are to be accurate and identify other alternative explanations. You can engage in dialogue with parts of yourself and give those parts empathy and understanding. For example, a part of you may be judging you for not completing a project perfectly. You can provide compassion to the part that is upset, disappointed, and angry at yourself for not continuing to edit a report you must turn in. We all have conditioned beliefs that may have once served us but may not do so now. It may have helped to strive to be a perfectionist when you were young in your family or at school, where you received praise for such attention to detail. However, your report is not being graded, and you will be better off not editing it for the tenth time. It is valuable to assess your thoughts and emotions to identify how accurate or realistic the underlying beliefs are for you at this time. Perhaps you don't need to strive for perfection for an internal memo. The obsessive behavior keeps you from other important issues. As you engage in dialogue with curiosity and non-

judgment, ideally, you experience relief from your strong emotions and cool down. You are then able to see more possibilities and be calmer.

Other ways to cool down include: taking a break such as a walk, breathing more deeply, counting to ten, meditating, becoming aware of sounds and sensations, getting empathy from a friend, recalling a beautiful scene where you felt relaxed such as at the beach or a forest, reading a book, or engaging in a favorite hobby such as gardening, listening to music, baking, being in nature, and assuming positive intent. If you judge someone, you might also try to cool down by writing a note expressing your view without sending the message. You might also seek other perspectives on a situation. Consider receiving empathy and understanding from a friend or a coach. When someone listens to us intently and cares about us, we experience connection and feel understood. We can more easily see different perspectives, and when we or someone understands our emotions, they more easily shift. One useful technique to regulate our nervous system is simply to sigh. You can hum or sing and also find humor and laugh to cool down. Remember to take care of yourself. Perhaps you need rest or healthy nutritious food, or even some fun to support you. I often tell myself to look for the opportunity and learning in a situation and expect things will work out somehow—even if I can't see how at the moment. I also challenge myself to make something positive out of what may appear to be negative.

Another resource for cooling down is to connect with your inner wise self. While a part of us is stressed, constricted, and ready to react, we can become aware of this resource that is more calm, more confident, and able to see different perspectives that we can call on. We can ask, "How would my wise or higher self see or approach this situation?" You can substitute any term that works for you, such as your kind or loving self, guide, sage, essence, love, peace, or joy.

It takes intention and practice to step back and cool down. And it is worth the effort. You will ultimately be less stressed and more capable of connecting with yourself, others, and possibilities. When you cool down, you are prepared to shift to being open. You move from contraction to expansion. When you can notice what is happening with a sense of respect and compassionate curiosity, you give space for blocked energy to shift. When energy is freed up, new possibilities and fuel for action emerge.

By stepping back, we can become more aware of the bigger picture and take in the situation. There are many ways to cool down. Experiment and discover what works best for you. Then keep a list on your phone, desk, or somewhere easily accessible to remind yourself of what helps you cool down. A critical action is to breathe deeply and fully. When we are contracted, we are often holding our breath, and our perception is limited.

3. Shift to Being Open.

When you have cooled down, you can allow yourself to shift to being open. Again, there are many strategies, so you need to find what best works for you. I find it useful to recall when I was open, such as when I was in Santorini, and to have those memories and sensations available. I have collected several such memories and related sensations. I can easily shift into such an oasis and reexperience being open. By oasis, I mean a place of rest and aliveness where you feel centered and renewed. I encourage you to take mental and real photos of such moments to let yourself experience the open flow. Notice what you are seeing, feeling, hearing, tasting, and smelling. When you engage your senses, you will experience the felt sense of being open. You can also create your own imagined oasis where you can be safe and open to possibilities. Another strategy is to imagine how your "ideal or wise self" would respond. I recall that my wise self would want to hear the facts before I reacted and jumped to conclusions. My ideal self intends to respond with grace rather than react when I feel upset, angry, or judgmental.

Take the perspective of a curious anthropologist. Stay open by being genuinely curious, compassionate, and interested in learning more about another perspective. Recall your sense of openness when you are genuinely eager to learn about something, such as a topic of interest or a person. I sometimes wonder how Nelson Mandela or Martin Luther King, Jr. might see a situation. I often remind myself to assume positive intent and shift to being curious.

Fortunately, your openness can be more than intellectual. Practice opening your heart and recalling a loved one such as a child or a pet, and notice how your heart feels in this open state. Put your hand on your heart, and feel it beating. Breathe into it to slow it down. Allow yourself to experience warmth and kindness. Be empathetic and understanding of yourself and others. Notice the free energy flowing through you.

Recall a time in the past when you felt centered and open as if in an oasis. Really allow all of your senses to reexperience the moment as I have done with my experience in Santorini. As you fully inhabit the experience, notice how your body changes. Perhaps you stand taller and your breathing slows. You may remember to shift into this body sculpture. You may add a phrase such as "ahh" that brings you to this open stance. I have often reconnected with being in Santorini and other places to shift my chemistry and emotions to being open. Create a metaphor or an image for being open and closed. For example, you can visualize a door, a faucet, a book, the gears of a car, or even a bridge opening and closing. You can assess how open the door or faucet is and what may support more opening.

You can shift to being open by focusing on any of the Open Stance Postures depicted in the model. When we are open, we experience being present and centered. You can breathe and feel your feet on the ground, notice the length of your spine, and bring your attention to the present moment and notice what you observe. You can recount what is going well with the situation and be optimistic about how things are unfolding. A surefire way of being open is to take a few minutes to reflect on all you are grateful for. Allow yourself to really experience the emotion of gratitude. What do you really appreciate about the person in front of you or your situation? Expect inspiration. You can ask for and expect guidance. You can call a friend and be authentic and connect. Appreciate the support you have received and consider how you can be more supportive. You can focus on what you appreciate about yourself, the person you are interacting with, or the situation. You can also take action to help others who may not be as fortunate as you. This will widen your perspective. You can focus on being curious and begin your statement with "I am curious to learn more." You can genuinely listen with the intent of understanding the other person, the situation, or even yourself. Remember to give a lot of empathy and to zip it up after you are empathetic. Be kind to yourself and others. Take a risk and share what you are feeling, and courageously try a new behavior. Appreciate yourself, others, and your situation, welcoming the learning that is possible. Focus on being considerate and taking kind action.

It is worthwhile to build a repertoire of experiences for each open stance. You will be able to recall and reexperience how you feel when you remember the support of a good friend who was there for you during a critical time. Notice how you feel calm and a warmth in your heart appreciating this connection. Allow that friendship to support you.

Now that you have noticed your constriction, have stopped, stepped back, and shifted to being open, you can consider a kind and healthy response. Rather than blaming, being judgmental, or jumping into a distraction, you can become centered and listen to others. You can refrain from being pessimistic and suggest options. You can remind yourself and others of what you have to be grateful for. Each situation will call for a different response. Ideally, you will consciously reflect on what will most support you, others, and the situation.

You can check in with yourself after your response to see how it feels for you. If you feel centered and positive, that is a clue you have been open. If you don't feel positive, you may reflect on what you can learn from the experience and consider other possible responses.

Awareness is the key. We can see and understand so much more when we are present, attentive, and open to learning and experimenting in a non-judgmental way. With practice, you will be able to identify if you are open and shift to being so. When you are open, you are primed for learning and adapting, and being effective with yourself and your interactions.

By building opportunities for renewal into our lives, we experience openness and activate our parasympathetic nervous systems. Research verifies that activities such as meditation, yoga, tai chi, prayer to a loving being, being hopeful, helping others, walking in nature, laughing and playfulness, stroking a pet, helping others, and listening to music are ways to renew and experience being open. We need to learn how to be comfortable with uncertainty. Play is a place where we can explore this sensation. Research suggests that doing these kinds of activities, often in small doses, is more impactful than just doing one thing for yourself occasionally. When we take responsibility for taking actions that support us in being open, we are better positioned to thrive and make a difference in others' lives since emotions are contagious. Recall Sarah's story when she was able to influence the negative relative to creating an open and positive atmosphere for a gathering.

Embodying an Open Stance

I have emphasized the value of being aware of your sensations to support you in noticing when you are open or closed. We each live in a body that experiences many sensations, and we are continually taking in new information. Also, we are giving information by the way we hold our bodies. In a study that colleagues and I did, we asked people when they were open and closed. Many said they immediately close based on the body language and mood of the person they interact with, often even before a person says anything. Almost at a preconscious level, we contract or mistrust people who seem closed, judgmental, or unsafe to us.

Try an experiment. Stand in a contracted posture with your shoulders rounded forward, your head down, and arms crossed. How do you feel? What is your mood? What are you thinking? Say, "I am curious, compassionate, and envisioning possibilities." How do you feel? Congruent? Do you think others will believe you with this body stance?

Take a deep breath and move around a bit. Now take an expansive posture. Spread your arms in a welcoming way, hold your head high, and smile. What are you experiencing from this embodiment? What is your mood? What are you thinking? Now say, "I am closed and not curious or open to new ideas." How does this feel? Congruent? I guess you don't feel congruent in either of these cases. Try an expansive posture and notice how you are feeling open and seeing possibilities.

Begin to notice how you are holding your body at different times and experiment with uncrossing your arms or legs and genuinely holding an open stance. Notice the relationship between your intentions, mood, and how you are holding your body. Notice what you are saying to yourself. Notice others. When are you likely to trust others and believe they are genuinely open? Remember the power of resonance. We are reading each other. The good news is our openness is contagious, so by being open, we can inspire others to be open.

Be Open to Yourself, Others, and the Situation

Are you open? Inquire often. This is one of the most important questions you can ask yourself. You could set a random timer on your phone to remind you to check in often with the question. It allows you to be present in the moment and make choices that will support you and others. You may intend to be open. However, we all have habitual patterns and hidden biases that affect our minds and hearts. It is just the way we are. Our experiences and background have affected us. We naturally protect ourselves by contracting and becoming closed to remain safe, to survive, and to maintain perceived control over our lives.

The Process of Shifting to Being Open / 77

In this closed state, we often miss positive connections and potential opportunities. Too often. We have a negativity bias and naturally see potential danger. However, when we recognize this, we can more consciously notice our immediate reactions and step back and cool down to shift to being open. We can apply the process of being open to ourselves, others, and our environment or situations. The same basic process can be used when we are in judgment.

First, we can focus on being open to ourselves. Part of the human condition is to experience challenges and suffering, as well as joyous moments. We each grew up in communities where there were expectations. To be effective and survive, we needed to conform and adjust in ways that may have cost us emotionally. Each of us has aspects of ourselves or parts that have developed from our experience. For example, we may have learned in our family to be very responsible and hide our feelings, or we may have felt we were not worthy or loved. We also have parts that want to be seen and other parts that make judgments. We know we are continually experiencing many emotions. When we are open to ourselves, we observe and appreciate our different parts in an accepting way. We trust that each of our emotions has a message for us. For example, a feeling of anger may be pointing to something we value and hold dear. We can learn to take responsibility for our emotions.

The observer part of us can have the intention to listen, be aware, and be open to our emotions. We can notice contractions and allow space for the feelings to convey their messages.

Several schools of thought emphasize a more extensive awareness that can observe and create space for our various feelings. Richard Schwartz developed Internal Family Systems, a process of attending to different emotions and allowing them to speak their needs and concerns. Another process, Focusing, initially developed by Eugene Gendlin, emphasizes experiencing the "felt sense" of emotions. Ann Weiser Cornell built on the work of Gendlin. She created interrelationship focusing where, again, a larger self in presence gives space for various sensations and emotions. Gestalt psychology and coaching also support being present to our emotions and stories. If we sense that we have multiple parts within us, the observer or present part of us can be open to each of our parts and hold that they are each doing the best they can based on their conditioning. When we create an inner space to be aware of our thoughts and emotions with compassionate curiosity, there is room for movement. We can experience more aliveness.

The Process of Shifting to Being Open / 79

When interacting with others, it is valuable to notice our signals of judgment or contractions. Then, rather than reacting, we can stop, step back, and shift into an open state of awareness and curiosity. Then we are positioned to listen with compassion and non-judgment. I share the OASIS process of interacting with others in my book, *OASIS Conversations: Leading with an Open Mindset to Maximize Potential*. Thousands have experienced the process in the *OASIS Conversations Course*. The OASIS moves involve being aware of our **O–O**bservation and what we are noticing. We separate our observations from our **A–A**wareness of our assumptions, emotions, and background. We then **S–S**hift to being open if we are contracted or in judgment—that is when we "know" we are right. We are then able to actively listen to the other party. We discover what is important to them, what is **I–I**mportant to us, and what is important to both of us—our common ground. We are then prepared to co-create **S–S**olutions and accountability. Many nuances exist when effectively conversing with another person or group. Being open to empathy and understanding is crucial.

We can apply the same process of being open to our external circumstances and environment. If we do not like our job or our neighborhood or community, we are likely to make judgments and become contracted. We can notice our signals of contraction and recall our intention to be open. We can stop reacting. Before taking action, we can step back and shift into a more curious and compassionate state. We can look for the learning and possibilities. This mindset may support us in managing our adverse reactions and discovering new opportunities. Actually, times of disruption and what may appear like negative situations are times when innovation is particularly possible. During the COVID-19 pandemic, while people were fearful, many were able to create new offerings and innovations.

I encourage you to create a shared vision with your family, team, organization, or community. For example, it would be powerful to inspire people to join together to take action, to create an open environment where people feel supported and creative, to engage in productive conversations, and to make life better for all involved. A shared vision where people join together with a felt sense of hope and aliveness can be compelling. It takes being in an open stance to see possibilities and have the energy to take action. The more people who practice open stances, the greater chance we have to achieve such compelling visions. When people join together for a shared purpose that is inspiring, much can happen. I envision the possibility of making the world better for all by spreading awareness of the benefits of adopting an open mindset and being open to the parts of ourselves, others, our situations, and the greater environment. When we are released from judgment and contraction, we experience a greater flow of energy and possibilities and are positioned to influence others and make a difference.

Closed/Open Continuum

We continue to move between being closed and open. The table below highlights some of the different aspects of each end of the continuum.

Closed	Open
judgmental	non-judgmental
reactive	responsive
view stress negatively	view stress positively as a challenge
contracted	expanded
maintains status quo	seeks creativity and innovation
resists change	welcomes change
controlling	seeks to understand what is evolving
blames others	takes responsibility
short-term thinking	longer-term thinking
focus on me	focus on we
desires certainty	comfortable with the unknown
sees a problem	sees opportunity
numbs feelings	honors feelings
not present	centered and present
pessimistic	optimistic
ungrateful	grateful
don't expect to be inspired	open to inspiration
not connected with others	connected with others
doesn't feel supported	receives support from others
negative assumptions	positive assumptions
not compassionate	compassionate and caring
not inviting	welcoming
risk averse	willing to take risks

We are continually opening and closing. The key is to become aware, and then we are more at choice about what actions we choose to take. Being flexible allows us to notice when we are reactive rather than responsive and then we can choose to be open or closed. As mentioned, we can close by not being grounded and present; by being pessimistic; by being negative, ungrateful, and closed to inspiration; or by not supporting and disconnecting from others. We can be closed-minded, harden our hearts, choose not to take risks, and choose not to take kind action. We can distract ourselves with many things, such as social media, shopping, eating, etc. We can easily slip into learned patterns of negative thoughts.

We have a cognitive tendency known as the confirmation bias that supports us in being closed-minded. It is natural to pay more attention to things that confirm our current beliefs and discount evidence that challenges our views. When we are aware of this human disposition, we can give ourselves time to consider alternative perspectives.

We close in the face of perceived danger, and this supports us in surviving. Closing can generate energy for change. We can consciously assess a situation and choose to be closed. With awareness, closing may be a healthy choice. You can take time for yourself and not be connected with others. You can recognize your negativity and use the experience to reflect on what is happening globally and determine appropriate action. You may then choose not to engage with others or an activity. In fact, we can't do everything, or we will easily become overwhelmed when we try. The key is being at choice with our actions. For example, I can be open to understanding a person's perspective, notice my contraction, and stop and learn more. However, I may ultimately choose to leave a job or a person or vote for a different candidate and work for a different solution. I can do these with choice and be open to the complexities and variety of options.

I can be open as I try to influence others to pursue different ways of living and being together. I can work against injustice in an open and curious state. When we close without awareness, we do not access the neocortex's creative capacity and limit our experience of resilience, wellbeing, and thriving.

A useful reflection is to check in regularly and notice if you are open or closed. You could give yourself a 5 on a 1-5 scale if you are fully open and a -5 on a -5 to -1 scale if you are fully closed. You could do this 5-8 times a day for a week and identify what is going on at the time. Then look at your scores and see if you notice any patterns. Are you mostly closed at work or with certain people? Are you open in the morning and closed in the afternoon? Identify what you may do to support yourself in a kind way. You want to be observant so you can easily shift to being open.

Are You Judging or Discerning?

It is our nature to judge ourselves and others. We each have an inner voice that accompanies us and tells us when things are not "right." When we are contracted or closed, we can be harsh in judging ourselves, others, and situations. Sometimes we call this judge our "inner critic" or saboteur. If you are like me, you may have many forms of this inner critic.

We can recognize our judgment when we hear that we or someone or something "should" be different. We sense in our bodies that we are "right" and others "should" agree. In addition to the berating inner voice, we usually have a predominant physical sensation that can be stronger depending on the issue. For example, I notice tension in my back, as if someone is pushing me, or a tightness in my stomach and a feeling of pressure.

We can use these signals to alert us that we are closed or judging. If we can shift to a more open stance, we can be less harsh and more curious or discerning.

For example, say you feel you did not do well on a presentation. You could notice your judging part saying things like, "You are a failure! You are not a good speaker; you never have been and never will be. Others are so much better." You may notice your signal and contraction. Your amygdala part of the brain is activated. If you can shift to a more open stance, you could more calmly assess the situation, learn from it, and determine your next steps. From an open state, you could see that you would have benefited by allowing more time for preparation and by practicing and getting support with the technology. You could learn from this experience, and you may even choose to hire a coach or take a course to improve your skills.

Discerning comes from an open and growth mindset. You recognize that we all can learn and develop. You are more centered, open, and compassionate. A discerning parent helps a child learn and recognizes that developing knowledge and skills takes time and ongoing improvement. Empathy and support exist in appreciating the child's intrinsic goodness and essence.

We can practice shifting into an open stance so we can be more discerning, support development, and value our intrinsic nature and that of others. We can learn to build the muscle of shifting to enjoy an open stance and continual growth. Practices for embodying an open stance are offered in the next section.

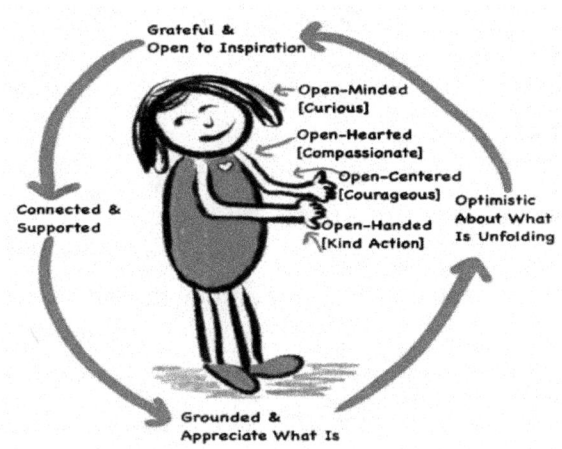

Part Three
Practices for Embodying an Open Stance

"Through practice, gently and gradually we can collect ourselves and learn how to be more fully with what we do."

— Jack Kornfield

THUS FAR, WE'VE TALKED ABOUT the benefits of being open and three simple steps to help us get there in the moment (Stop, Step Back, and Shift to being open). Ideally, as we practice these steps, we build the neural pathways and habit of noticing our contraction and reaction to differences and shifting to being open.

According to James Clear, author of *Atomic Habits*, the key to building lasting habits is focusing on identity first. For example, view yourself as a runner rather than just setting a goal to run three miles each day. Our behaviors are a reflection of our current identity and the type of person we believe we are. The way to change our behavior is to start believing new things about ourselves. Ideally, you begin seeing yourself as someone who takes an open stance. You are an open person who is self-aware and able to shift to being open to others, yourself, situations, new ideas, and taking kind actions in the world. With this identity, you can take small steps such as recalling and experiencing the components of an open stance and focusing on building your open stance muscles in an area such as keeping a journal of what you are grateful for each day.

Now we need to explore some strategies that will help us stay in that open stance so it ultimately becomes our way of being. You can review each of the practices as you set your intention, or just focus on one at a time. It is helpful to remember the blind spot that others may not perceive us as being as open as we think we are. This is why it is useful to recall our intention and the various aspects of being open.

A book could be written on each stance, so I encourage you to learn more about each. Our purpose in this book is to highlight the components of an open stance and offer practices to help support openness.

Open Stance Postures

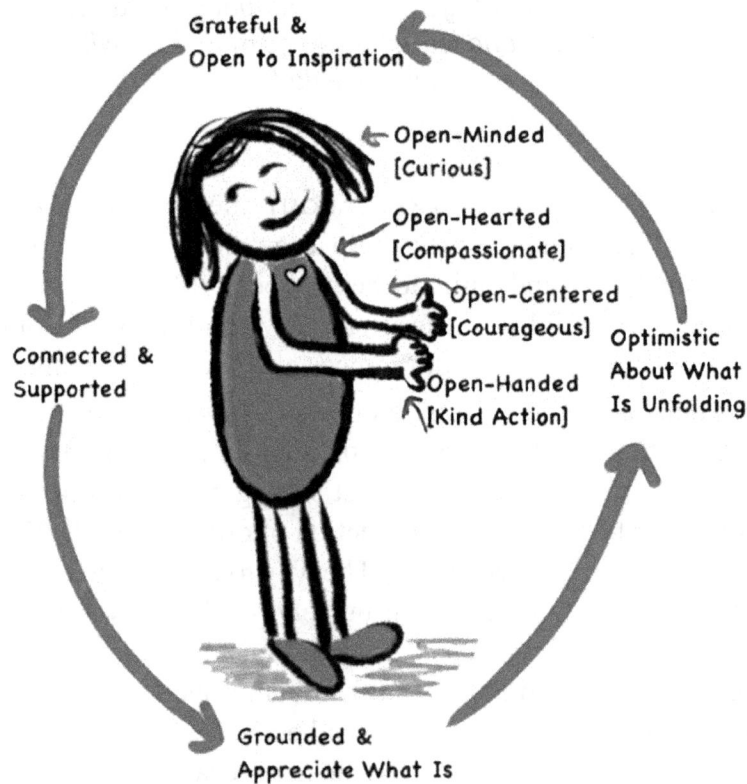

The Open Stance Postures model (above) is intended to serve as a guide in helping you become more fully self-aware and purposeful in your quest to be open. You may begin by exploring how you position yourself and relate to the external environment; that is, what it means to feel *grounded* and fully present in the moment. Once there, you are more able to assess what is unfolding before you with intentional *optimism*. Even when you question what's to come, the idea is to seek out the good. This, in turn, flows right into *gratitude* for all you have and the inspiration and creativity it evokes. Finally, the benefit of feeling *connected and supported* by relationships is essential in the face of challenges.

To go deeper, you can examine internally if you are *open-minded, open-hearted, open-centered,* and/or *open-handed*? What is unique about this model is that each focal point is a place for reflection, a place to pause and get clear about where you are. For me, there is a logical sequence, but it is not necessary to follow it. I happen to like imagining the model and literally following and feeling each of the focal points in my own body. Because this process has become a habit for me, I can do the full-body "scan" in a minute. I often rely on it as a means of starting my day and confirming my intention to be open. I invite you to use this model in the best way that suits you. I will walk you through how it works for me.

Visualize your embodied self and imagine setting your intention to the following:

- » Be Grounded and Appreciate What Is—This is a way of saying be present in the moment; breathe deeply [feel your feet on the ground; appreciate what is]
- » Be Optimistic about What Is Unfolding—Imagine a positive outcome to what is unfolding [look forward and envision a favorable future]
- » Be Grateful and Open to Inspiration—Focus on what you appreciate; trust intuition and creativity [look up]
- » Be Connected—Receive and give support; connect with yourself, others, and the environment [notice and touch your

back and envision a community of interconnections and support behind you]

In addition, imagine the physical/spiritual parts of yourself (heart, mind, hands, and core center) that will guide you in your intention to be open:

- » Be Open-Minded—Curious/non-judgmental [touch your head and be aware of thoughts]
- » Be Open-Hearted—Compassionate/empathetic [put your hand on your heart]
- » Be Open-Centered—Courageous/vulnerable [put your hand on your belly]
- » Be Open-Handed—Taking kind action such as welcoming, accepting, and being respectful [open your hands]

Sense what it feels like to be open in your body. You can imagine opening your heart (metaphorically) and giving empathy to yourself. You can use your body to remind you of the various ways you can become open and focus on any one of these areas as a doorway to becoming more open. It will be useful to recall moments when you experienced being optimistic, grateful, connected, etc. As you recall those moments, allow yourself to reexperience the sensations so you have a full-body experience. This will allow you to move quickly to the experience of being open.

You can learn more about how to engage in productive relationships and conversations by being open in my book *OASIS Conversations: Leading with an Open Mindset to Maximize Potential.*

Identify times or places where you can check in on yourself and notice how open you are. You can ask, "Am I open? Open-hearted? Open-handed?"

Practice and Reinforcement

"Let go of certainty. The opposite isn't uncertainty. It's openness, curiosity and willingness to embrace paradox."

—Tony Schwartz

Practices for Embodying an Open Stance / 89

Consciously commit to adopting an open mindset and then reminding yourself of the stances of being open. For example, you may walk through the stances and visualize being curious, compassionate, and courageous. Make it a habit to review the stances each morning or as you transition from one activity to another.

Place reminders where you will see them that encourage you to pause and reflect, "Are you open?" I sometimes have the letters RUOPN? as a reminder on my desk or notepad. When I notice them, I take a moment to check-in and shift to being open.

Have a friend or a coach support you in this process. You may find it helpful to keep a journal with your reflections and to learn more about each stance.

Research on neuroscience and mindfulness suggests we can actually change our brain's structure and, thus, how we see and interact in the world.[27] Rick Hanson, a respected psychologist, suggests we can build states into traits through experience-dependent neuroplasticity.[28] What we repeatedly sense, feel, and focus on begins to sculpt our neural structure. There is a famous saying: *Neurons that fire together, wire together.* For example, research shows that London taxi drivers have thickened neural layers in their hippocampus. This brain region makes visual-spatial memories, which help them easily maneuver the complex London streets. In the same way, meditators build a thicker cortex and more easily relax. As you focus on the open stances and experience being optimistic, grateful, curious, and empathetic, your brain will build the groove for these ways of being. Then you will more easily and naturally experience being open.

Rick Hanson also suggests that if we savor positive experiences by focusing on them, we prolong and enrich them, which heightens their absorption into our emotional memory. We will build the neural pathways to experience these emotions more readily. I suggest you recall moments when you have experienced the open stances and revisit them often, even for a few moments. When you do so, you can remind yourself of your intention to be open and strengthen your neural pathways.

It is best to engage often in small practices than to engage occasionally in longer ones. For example, reviewing and imagining using each of the stances in the morning and the evening will serve you better than meditating once a week for a more extended period.

I encourage you to use your body sensations as a reminder to recall your intention to be open. By practicing, you are confirming your commitment. It is also useful to reflect on how you have exhibited the stances in the past. For example, you may realize you recently

---

27. Siegel, D. J. *The Developing Mind: How Relationships and the Brain Interact to Shape Who We Are.* 2nd ed. New York, NY: Guilford Press, 2012.
28. https://www.rickhanson.net/growing-good/

Practices for Embodying an Open Stance / 91

showed empathy with a coworker. You may recall being optimistic before a team meeting. You may have felt your feet on the ground and been present for a conversation with a family member. It is helpful to reflect on such occurrences so you will begin to associate them with being open.

Below is an Open Stance Postures Self-Reflection. Identify which area you would like to develop.

The sections after the Open Stance Postures Reflection will explore each of the postures and offer further practice suggestions to develop the open stances. Notice which practices appeal to you and experiment with those.

Open Stance Postures Reflection

Rate yourself on a scale from -5 to +5 on how you embody each of the stances. A +5 indicates that you often or to a strong degree embody the stance. For example, you are very grateful. A negative score indicates that you are low on embodying the stance. For example, a -5 means you are definitely not grateful.

Then, identify any Open Stances that you would like to enhance.

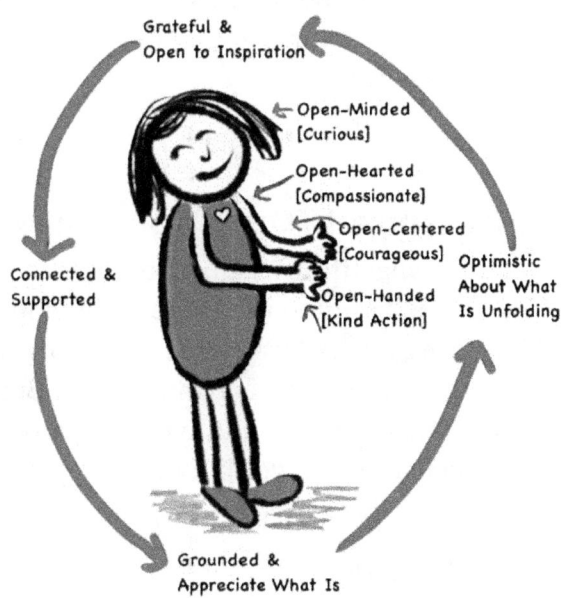

Open Stance Self-Reflection

===

Grounded and Appreciate *What Is* (Open to the Present)

Being fully present (feet on the ground) in your body and connected with the earth. Allowing yourself to feel centered and balanced, regardless of circumstances. Noticing your senses (what you see, hear, feel). Paying attention to breathing. Being aware and managing distractions. Engaging with what is happening in the moment rather than worrying about the past or the future. Noticing new things and paying attention to details.

-5   -4   -3   -2   -1   0   +1   +2   +3   +4   +5

Optimistic About What Is Unfolding (Open to the Future)

Being hopeful and resilient. Accepting change. Trusting that things will work out, even when not clear how. Focusing on positivity, potential, and possibilities. Finding the gifts in situations and people. Believing that good things will happen. Looking at the bright side and expecting positive outcomes.

-5   -4   -3   -2   -1   0   +1   +2   +3   +4   +5

Grateful and Inspired (Open to Creative Flow)

Deeply appreciating what life offers; i.e., the earth, health, wellbeing, skills, food, friends, job, differences, etc. Noticing the good and inspirational. Not taking things for granted. Listening for new insights and connections. Enjoying creating and innovating. Being thankful for .... Expecting insights and making intuitive connections. Experiencing positivity and a sense that life is worth living. Experiencing a creative flow.

-5   -4   -3   -2   -1   0   +1   +2   +3   +4   +5

Connected and Supported (Open to Back-Up Support)

Recognizing your connectedness to others, yourself, and the environment. Appreciating interconnectedness. Building and maintaining relationships. Knowing that others are there to lend support. Believing you belong to a larger world and are not alone. Looking for common ground and interests. Building diverse and inclusive communities. Actualizing your values and being aware of what's meaningful and important to you.

-5   -4   -3   -2   -1   0   +1   +2   +3   +4   +5

Curious (Open-Minded)

Inquisitive thinking. Wondering what something is about. Investigating, exploring, learning. Wanting to know more and to understand. Being open to *what is* without judgment. Letting go of being *right* and being willing to be surprised. Becoming comfortable with "not knowing." Adapting a sense of playfulness to discover new things. Assuming positive intent.

-5   -4   -3   -2   -1   0   +1   +2   +3   +4   +5

Compassionate (Open-Hearted)

Attuned to what others are experiencing. Putting yourself in the place of another. Finding empathy for those who are, act, think, feel and look different. *Seeing* with the heart and being kind. Sensitive to the pain or misfortune of others. Caring about our own and others' wellbeing. Being compelled to take action—to make a difference and alleviate suffering. Recognizing that being imperfect, failing, and experiencing life's difficulties is inevitable.

-5   -4   -3   -2   -1   0   +1   +2   +3   +4   +5

Courageous (Open-Centered)

Allowing oneself to be vulnerable. Sharing who you are from the inside out. Being aware of your sensations and impulses and sharing your experience authentically. Not deterred by pain or obstacles. Adaptable. Assessing risk and stepping forward. Overcoming fears. Taking a stand on values and confronting adversity. Speaking from the heart. Creating an environment for others to be vulnerable and take risks. Sensing you are "enough." Forgiving ourselves and others.

-5   -4   -3   -2   -1   0   +1   +2   +3   +4   +5

Take Kind Action (Open-Handed)

Being responsive. Reaching out to others in need or in friendship—to connect, to lend a hand, to provide resources, to touch. Seeking ways to be inclusive and equitable, as an individual or a community. Creating space for differences. Engaging in respectful and welcoming action to influence and make the world better for all. Taking care of yourself and finding how you can best contribute using your insight, talent, and skills.

-5   -4   -3   -2   -1   0   +1   +2   +3   +4   +5

The Open Stance Posture I plan to focus on is:

_____

_____

In addition to focusing on one or two Stances to develop, rate where you are on your ability to Shift to Being Open, which is the process of moving from a Closed to an Open Stance.

Shift to Being Open (Mental Fitness Muscle)

Noticing contraction and judgment toward ourselves, others, or a situation and intending to Stop, Step Back, and Shift to Being Open. Stopping ourselves from reacting or closing and allowing space to cool down. Exploring ways to cool down, such as taking time away from a situation, receiving empathy, or engaging in another activity. Shifting into an expansive state of being open where we can be choiceful in our response.

-5   -4   -3   -2   -1   0   +1   +2   +3   +4   +5

Practices for Embodying an Open Stance / 95

I will enhance my mental fitness by:

_____
_____
_____
_____
_____

Be Grounded and Present and Appreciate What Is

Be Grounded—experience being present and appreciate what is
[sense your feet on the ground and be present]
"Be where you are; otherwise you will miss your life."
— Buddha

To be open, you need to be present and attuned to your body rather than being caught in the trance of your thoughts. Rather than reacting to people and situations, you can choose to observe your sensations, thoughts, and emotions. With this awareness, you can be "at choice" about what you say and do. Think about how young children are fully present in the moment. They are not worrying about the past or the future; they engage with what is in front of them. They naturally respond to sensations in their bodies and let caregivers know when they are cold, hungry, or playful.

Being grounded is a practice that connects your body to the earth (metaphorically). The term suggests balance and strength. To be grounded is closely associated with being fully present. It is as if your body is lodged in place (picture a tree with roots), and you're in a state of conscious awareness. As adults, many of us tend to live in our thoughts and worries. Research suggests we are focused on the past or future about half the time, rather than being in the moment. It can almost seem that our bodies are merely there to carry our heads around. When I used to feel like a bobbing head, I failed to benefit from the messages and sense of aliveness available from the rest of my body.

When we are engrossed in our thoughts, we miss much information. Also, by focusing on the past or future, many experience depression or anxiety. We miss opportunities to experience the joy and aliveness of the present moment.

As noted earlier, research supports the value of being mindful, being aware of our sensations, and reconnecting with our bodies. Too many of us feel like we are running fast these days. It is as if we are racing to take life in. Without awareness of our bodies, we are merely going through the motions. We feel drained. When we are grounded in our bodies, we can become centered, calm, and relaxed.

According to Ellen Langer, too many of us are "not there." When we are "not there," we don't realize we are not present. Simply noticing new things and being attentive supports you in being present. A great practice is to routinely bring your attention to what you are actually experiencing. For example, feel your seat on the chair and notice various sounds such as traffic, a horn, and someone's voice. Notice the sensation of tightening a muscle. Focus on sensations you are experiencing in the moment.

Jon Kabat-Zinn, creator of Stress Reduction Clinic and Center for Mindfulness in Medicine, Healthcare, and Society at University of Massachusetts Medical School, is a strong proponent of mindfulness meditation as a means of being in the present moment and regulating emotions. According to Kabat-Zinn, "mindfulness practice means that we commit fully in each moment to be present,"[29] paying attention to what is, which ultimately leads to calmness and equanimity right here and now.

Presence in others captures our attention like a magnet. We are aware of when someone is present in the moment. We experience resonance where we feel aligned and mutually energized. While useful at times, our habitual patterns can cause us to leap into action or turn away before fully realizing a situation, and thus, we lose the opportunity to be fully present and aware.

Many ways exist to become more present and attuned to our bodies and sensations. You can engage in simple experiments to feel more present, centered, and in your body. The key is to focus your attention on your sensations to enable you to experience being present rather than being lost in your thoughts. Here are some methods to try:

» Imagine that roots extend into the ground through your feet and spread out beneath the ground or floor. Imagine the energy from the earth coming through the roots and reaching up through you. This practice will help you feel present and grounded.

» Place your attention on your feet and feel them tapping the ground as you walk. Notice how your left foot feels and then how your right foot feels. Do you notice a sense of tingling and the flow of energy? I encourage executives I coach to pay attention to their feet as they walk from one meeting to the next and to clear their minds as they leave a meeting. Noticing their feet and taking a breath of air is like removing the space from one event and stepping into the present.

---

29. https://www.mindfulnesscds.com

- Become aware of what you are experiencing with your senses of seeing, hearing, smelling, touching, and feeling. Stay with the sensation for 10-15 seconds to strengthen the process. For example, rather than worrying or planning, notice the hot water temperature and the pressure of the water flow in the shower, and smell the fresh coffee. Expand your moments of being present. Make it a habit of checking in to capture what you notice. Studies have linked focused attention on present physical sensations with the parts of the brain that support being open.

- Take a deep belly breath. If you observe a baby or an animal in a calm state, you will notice their stomach expands and contracts as they breathe. Many of us breathe more shallowly in our upper chest. This shallow breathing tells our brain to prepare for a fight-or-flight response. However, when we take deep breaths, we send the message that we are in a calm state, and we can rest and rejuvenate.

- Put a hand on your stomach and the other on your chest. Inhale deeply and allow your belly to fill with air, like a balloon. You should notice your lower hand on your stomach move. Hold that breath for a moment, then fully exhale. (It should take about twice the amount of time as the inhale.) Allow yourself naturally to take in more air. Practice this pattern a few times and notice your enhanced awareness of being in the present. You can then return to normal breathing and observe the rise and fall of your abdomen. You can do this during meetings, while you wait in line, or when you take a break. You can then check in at various times to notice and calm your breath and observe your present circumstances.

- Take a few moments to scan your body, starting at your head, feet, or any part of your body, and notice what you experience. Envision it as shining a flashlight on you to analyze your sensations. You can spend two minutes scanning your whole body or take an hour for the process. You can stop and give attention to parts that are tight or constricted. Ideally, you will become aware of the flow of energy, recognize where you are, and be open to your situation.

» Contract your muscles very tightly (your eyes, face, belly, arms, and legs) and hold the tension. Then slowly release the pressure and relax. You can even sigh aloud as you release. Notice your sensations and allow yourself to experience the moment.

» Practice centering yourself. Stand tall and notice your length; appreciate your spine and experience a sense of identity. Notice your width and recognize your connections with others. Notice your depth, feel the front and back of your body, and connect with your past and future. Connect with your purpose and experience the energy of your vision. Notice what it is like to be centered.

» Reverse the order of things you do habitually. Take a beginner's mindset. Brush your teeth with the other hand. Change the order of how you get dressed, i.e., put your socks on first if you usually do so last.

» Give yourself reminders to be present. Build habits such as becoming aware of your breath and body sensations as you go from one room to the next, hear the phone ring, wait for a stoplight, or stand in line. Just check in to become aware that you have a body and that you are present in the moment. Be sure not to judge your body, but give it compassionate, curious awareness as if you were shining a flashlight on it for attention.

» Set a random timer and reconnect with being present. Allow yourself to sink into the feeling of being grounded each time you are alerted. Appreciate that you are building "muscles" of shifting your attention to the present. This supports you in being open.

» Have a clear sense of purpose or mission; it also serves to ground you. You know what is important to you and can stay centered.

» Feel the ground below you and ask yourself: "Am I open to being grounded and present?"

"If there were no night, we would not appreciate the day, nor could we see the stars and the vastness of the heavens. We must partake of the bitter and the sweet. There is divine purpose in the adversities we encounter every day. They prepare, they purge, they purify, and thus they bless."

— James E. Faust

Now that you are present to what is and are experiencing sensations in your body rather than being consumed with thoughts about the past, future, or what should be, you can take in and experience appreciation for something in your life. Even if it is a small thing such as where you live, allow yourself to experience appreciation.

You often hear people who have a life-threatening illness report that they appreciate life—experiencing appreciation and joy for each moment. They have a heightened awareness of beauty and connections.

Being appreciative is a powerful emotion. It is a feeling of thankfulness. Perhaps you appreciate watching a beautiful sunset, seeing children playing, eating a delicious meal, or having a pleasant conversation with a friend. Research by HeartMath[30] demonstrates that your heart rhythms are more congruent when you are in a positive, appreciative state. Also, your immune system is robust, and you experience an overall state of wellbeing. This sense of appreciation for what is before you is contagious and allows you and others to relax. In some ways, time seems to slow down.

Focusing on appreciation for yourself, others, or situations is a great way to be open. The more you begin to notice the positive things in your life, the easier it will become. You will experience more openness and joy when you can let go of past and future worries and focus on the current moment. Even when you notice your habitual patterns of judgment and struggle, you can catch yourself and recognize the peace of the here and now. Your intention to stay in the moment allows you to access ease.

We know things are always changing in our lives and the world. It is human nature to resist change and the unknown. Many leaders spend a lot of time and energy trying to convince people of the need to change. Typically, resistance has to do with uncertainty of where the change will lead and what it will mean. Again, when we can access the ease of the present moment, it allows us to accept what's to come more readily.

Arnold Beisser, a psychiatrist, writes about the paradoxical theory of change, which is a Gestalt concept.[31] The theory holds that if we

---

30. www.heartmath.org
31. Beisser, A. "The Paradoxical Theory of Change." In *Gestalt Therapy Now: Theories, Techniques, Applications.* eds. Joen Fagan and Irma Lee Shepherd. Gouldsboro, ME: Gestalt Journal Press, 2006. 77-80.

first accept and appreciate *what is*, the change will more naturally evolve. When you begin to recognize *what is*, you will experience less resistance, and there will be more energy for change. Appreciating *"what is"* is quite powerful and a useful component of the open stance. Given our propensity for a negativity bias, we can easily fall into the pattern of complaining, blaming, trying to control, and wanting things to be different. It is easy to find what is missing or wrong even during a picnic on a sunny day (maybe the bugs?). You can appreciate *"what is"* without being happy or liking it. For example, let's say it unexpectedly rains on your picnic. You definitely don't like that it's raining, but you can still appreciate that you're with your friends or that it's still warm despite the rain.

Much work in organizations has shown the power of Appreciative Inquiry, developed by David Cooperrider.[32] Rather than ask what the problems were, consultants used the Appreciative Inquiry approach to ask people what was going well and what they appreciated about their team or organization. The appreciation question shifted energy to finding the teams' strengths and formed a basis upon which to build.

Our moods quickly shift like the weather. By making it a practice of noticing what is happening in the moment and appreciating it, we build the skill of being in the moment. We then see that all sorts of thoughts will come and go, but we are alive and available.

The simple act of appreciating *what is* helps us to see and experience the present moment. Rather than rushing to put dinner on the table and complaining to ourselves or others about the task, we can acknowledge that we have food, a family, health, and a home. We can connect with a stillness that we easily miss when we get lost in thoughts about what we have to do and what is not working.

To build the muscle of appreciating *what is*, try some of the following practices and create your own.

» Make it a practice to focus on the miracles all around you for a few minutes each day. Take a five-minute walk, ideally out in

---

32. Cooperrider, D. L. *The Appreciative Inquiry Handbook: For Leaders of Change.* San Francisco: Berrett-Koehler Publishers, 2008.

nature, each day with this purpose and notice your experience of awe and appreciation.

- Make it a habit to express appreciation for the present moments. Share your appreciation with those around you.

- Notice when you most experience being in the moment with joy. I experience being in the present when I am coaching leaders and teams and working with groups. I seem to lose a sense of time and enjoy the creative moments. I feel energized and fully myself. Find your times of being present and create more of those experiences.

- Keep a journal or notice daily moments of joy. This will support you in paying attention throughout the day.

- Work on extending your appreciation to the positive moments and challenging moments when you are attending to yourself and others and not worrying about the past or future.

- Set a timer on your computer or phone, or pick a time such as every hour, and note what is happening and appreciate *what is*. Build the muscle of appreciating *what is*. Notice your experience.

- Put your hand on your chest and be present and notice without judgment. You may become aware of the sensation and warmth of your hand. Just be present. Allow five minutes a day to be still and appreciate what is.

- Identify moments when you relax and appreciate *"what is."* Perhaps you enjoy nature, music, a cup of tea, a bath, or stretching. Make a commitment to build such moments into your day.

- Consciously slow down to live and experience the actual moment. Create space in your day to be rather than filling every hour with activity.

- Avoid multitasking and make a choice to do something. Focus on one thing rather than letting your mind wander into the future or trying to do too many things at once.

- » Say an affirmation: I am grounded and appreciate *what is*.
- » Feel the ground below you and ask yourself: "Am I open to appreciating '*what is*'?"

Be Optimistic About What Is Unfolding

Be optimistic about what is unfolding
[look forward and envision a positive future]

*"I've had a lot of worries in my life,
most of which never happened."*

— Mark Twain

Do you trust that things will work out and that you and others will be okay? I know that is hard to do in such a turbulent and disordered world. Our brains have evolved with a tendency toward fear and unease. We tend to scan our environments for signs of trouble. While this perspective is understandable, our worry takes energy and interrupts our sense of resilience and wellbeing. It is useful to notice our anxious thoughts and recognize it is human nature to be concerned in the face of uncertainty. We can then adopt an optimistic view of possibilities (with the realism that we can't predict the future).

Optimism may be simply defined as both a personality trait and a learned ability related to positive expectations for the future. It is an outlook, a point of view, an orientation toward life that focuses on the positive. To be optimistic is a practice that comes naturally to some and must be developed in others. For example, some people maintain optimism even under the direst circumstances. Others who "have it all" can only focus on the downside. Closely related to appreciating what is, optimism is being positive about what is unfolding. Becoming optimistic is a goal worth pursuing. It can be developed.

When we are open to what is unfolding, it is easier to accept change and more readily surrender to circumstances outside of our control. Rather than seeing change as threatening, we take it as an inevitable part of life. We know we are continually growing and evolving. We also grow in confidence as we handle the many challenges life offers.

How often are we in real danger? Are you not more okay than not? Of course, there are challenges. That will always be a part of life. And yet, can you sense being mostly all right? How do you want to live? Where do you side on Einstein's view that you either consider life a miracle or not?

If you ponder it, you can see how life has been unfolding in miraculous ways. How does an acorn know to grow into an oak tree? How does our body know to heal after a cut? We know that generally, with time, the healing will occur. Fortunately, there have probably been more positive things evolving for many of us than not in our lives.

Research shows that those who adopt an optimistic view tend to be more successful and more satisfied. Martin Seligman, a well-known researcher on optimism, found that optimistic life insurance agents outsold others. Those who are optimistic tend to be happier and healthier, have better careers, make more money, and have better relationships. According to Seligman, when we tackle the cognitive distortions of personalization, pervasiveness, and permanence, we can learn to be optimistic.[33]

I know that most of what I have worried about in my life has not come to fruition or at least not been as bad as I imagined. Psychologists believe we can adopt a stance of optimism; it can be a learned ability.

I encourage you to experiment with the view that things are unfolding for good, and then trust and look for positive outcomes. I trust that no matter how things turn out, I will find meaning and learn. I trust I will be able to learn and grow from each experience. I look for the positive in the challenges I face. I often enjoy imagining that things are transpiring in a good way. If a meeting gets canceled, I look for the gift in that and what emerges. Perhaps I will meet someone else and learn something. Countless clients have shared with me how they seemed to have been in the right place at the right time for a positive outcome to emerge. And I would argue that that can only happen when one is open to seeing the bright side or finding the silver lining.

Sometimes it takes a while for things to "work out," and only later can we see the benefit of our journey. Many authors, such as those of the *Chicken Soup for the Soul* series, share stories of their books being rejected more than a hundred times before becoming bestsellers. Michael Jordan was cut from his high school basketball team, and Walt Disney was fired from his newspaper job since he was perceived to be lacking ideas. Both later became successful leaders in their fields. Each reported the benefits of their complicated process to success. How would life be different if we were more trusting of the process?

Expecting that the effort you put into studying or a project will pay off or anticipating that you will have an affirming day can increase the likelihood that you will. Some refer to this as the "power of positive thinking." The expectancy or placebo effect is well documented. A landmark study by Jon Levine in 1978 suggested that patients don't

---

33. https://positivepsychology.com/learned-optimism/

just imagine their pain lessens with a placebo. Still, there is actual measurable change with placebos mediated by the release in the brain of endogenous opioids called endorphins. Placebos can activate endorphins and dopamine, which dilates blood vessels and affects the response to pain. "Placebos can modulate the same chemical pathways that are modulated by drugs."[34]

Many subsequent brain imaging studies show the power of expectancy with related physical changes in the brain.[35] Expecting positive outcomes is likely to generate positive results. Of course, if you expect things not to work out, you are also likely to realize your expectations. Your expectations will influence your thoughts and actions.

Positive thinking contributes to greater health, productivity, and happiness. Recall the classical Taoist story of the farmer who faced many challenges. First his horse runs away. His neighbors come over to give him empathy, "We're so sorry about your horse." The farmer replies "Who knows what's good or bad?" The neighbors are confused since the horse is so valuable and critical for survival. The horse comes back a few days later with a group of feral horses. The neighbors congratulate the farmer on his great fortune. The farmer replies again, "Who knows what's good or bad?" While the farmer's son is taming the wild horses, he's thrown off of a horse and breaks his leg. Again the neighbors offer their condolences. The farmer again responds, "Who knows what's good or bad?" Next, the army comes through and conscripts able-bodied young men to fight in war. The farmer's son is spared because of his broken leg. The story proceeds in this manner. Taking a larger perspective enables us to be open to what is possible.

» Practice acting as if things are unfolding positively. Look with anticipation and expectation that possibilities will materialize.

» Brainstorm at least three opportunities in a situation that first appears negative. For example, perhaps losing a big client will

---

34. Levine, J. D., Gordon, N. C. and Fields, H. L. "The Mechanism of Placebo Analgesia." *The Lancet.* 312.8091 (1978): 654-57.
35. Marchant, J. "Placebos: Honest Fakery." *Nature.* 535.7611 (2016): S14-15. http://nature.com/nature/journal/v535/n7611_supp/full/535S14a.html#ref3.

give you time to develop an even better product and eventually gain even more clients.

» Be hopeful. When asked how he was able to survive a dreadful childhood foster care experience while his brother ended up in prison, the young African-American author of *Finding Fish*, Antoine Fisher, responded "imagination." He was always able to imagine a better life for himself. He never lost hope.

» Look for life events you initially interpreted as negative that you now see evolved into positive outcomes. Write about these events and perhaps make a list of the benefits of challenging situations in your life. For example, it was a challenging work situation that led me to study leadership and work with leaders. If I had not needed college funds, I would not have had the benefit of years of working experience and related growth.

» Notice when you feel worried about the future and try to calm that part of you that is concerned. I know this is not easy since the world faces so many collective challenges. Recall how you have fared well amid many challenges. And give yourself the encouragement you need to break through your discouragement.

» Dare to expand your views about what is possible, and never lose faith that you will prevail in the long term.

» Make it a practice of looking for positive outcomes in what may initially seem like an adverse event. Practice finding the silver lining. Collect these stories to remind yourself that you don't know how something will turn out.

» Practice visualizing positive outcomes for your day. Shift to positive thoughts and expectations. Set a time when you visualize regularly and allow your body to sense positive results.

» Imagine how someone with an optimistic perspective would see things.

» Make it a daily practice to reflect on what is working well.

Practices for Embodying an Open Stance / 109

- » Befriend optimistic people and practice adopting their perspectives.
- » Take care of yourself. It is hard to focus on possibilities when you are tired and low on energy.
- » See yourself as a resilient and competent person who is strong, resourceful, and capable of learning. Remind yourself of this.
- » Seek other perspectives from mentors, advisors, and trusted resources.
- » Practice sharing positive outcomes to situations.
- » Reflect on what gives you hope and notice where in your body you experience hope and optimism.
- » Keep a journal of moments of joy each day and notice the patterns. For example, you may see that you experience joy when with friends or in nature.
- » Notice how you experience life when you act as if the glass is half-full.
- » Experiment with the idea that things are unfolding beneficially and look for the learning in events.
- » Write positive affirmations and review them regularly.
- » Savor positive moments and keep a list or pictures of such moments to remind yourself of what's possible. Relive positive moments.
- » Maintain positive momentum even when life presents challenges. Look for what you can learn and how you are growing through these experiences. Recognize that the challenges are a part of life that all humans go through.
- » When you notice your negative thoughts, reflect on whether they are helpful, and try to reframe. If you are not optimistic about a meeting or family gathering, look for the benefits.
- » Notice if you are negatively comparing yourself to others. Recognize that these comparisons are not improving your

life. You can't really know what is going on for others, even if things look good for them.

» Take care of your energy with healthy food, adequate sleep, and time for relaxation and physical activity.

» Smile often. Studies suggest that smiling can make you feel more optimistic about the present and future. Spend time on things that make you smile or laugh.

» Look forward and ask yourself: "Am I open to being optimistic that things are unfolding positively?"

Be Grateful and Open to Inspiration

Be grateful and open to inspiration—
experience thankfulness, trust intuition and creativity [look up]

> *"Gratitude can transform common days into thanksgivings, turn routine jobs into joy, and change ordinary opportunities into blessings."*
> — William Arthur Ward

By now, you are likely to have heard of the many benefits of being grateful. You will experience more inner ease, notice more good moments, and connect more easily to others. Not bad.

From a scientific perspective, gratitude is more than the act of saying thanks; it is also a positive emotion. According to Courtney Ackerman at positivepsychology.com, "Positive psychology defines gratitude in a way where scientists can measure its effects, and thus argue that gratitude is more than feeling thankful; it is a deeper appreciation of someone (or something) that produces longer lasting positivity."[36] However, it is not enough to have a gratitude journal or casually identify that for which you are thankful. Ideally, you build the habit and neural pathway of noticing gratitude and inspiration. You will benefit from actually experiencing gratitude in your body. For example, you may feel warmth in your chest or heart area because you are grateful for a child or friend or job. We often focus on what we don't have or what could go wrong, and then we experience more fear and anxiety.

We need to build the habit of expecting serendipity, intuition, surprises, and creativity. This is especially important during these periods of unprecedented disruption and change. We can continually notice and appreciate the good around us. Our emotions are contagious. Our gratefulness and openness to inspiration can enable others to be open to possibilities.

We can build the habit of being grateful and open to inspiration. Studies support the power of an "attitude of gratitude." For example, in one study, participants were asked to write letters of gratitude. The study reported positive changes in their behavior and higher activity in the brain's medial prefrontal cortex up to three months later.[37] Practicing gratitude activates positivity in the brain. Research supports

---

36. Ackerman, C. "What Is Gratitude and Why Is It So Important?" positivepsychology.com/gratitude-appreciation. May 2, 2021.
37. Kini, P. et al. "The Effects of Gratitude Expression on Neural Activity." *NeuroImage*. 128 (2016): 1-10. https://www.ncbi.nlm.nih.gov/pubmed/2674580

that being thankful increases our use of imagination and our ability to problem-solve, and it enhances health and longevity.[38]

Studies suggest that gratitude is a key to health and happiness. Being grateful and open to inspiration and new ideas helps us connect to the larger world and feel that life is worth living. I had to consciously work on noticing what I was grateful for and being open to creative inspiration and new ideas. I will never forget waking up one night and experiencing gratitude for my life rather than my old pattern of worry and fretting about what I needed to do and what I didn't have. I developed the habit of being grateful, and it made a big difference for me and those around me.

I associate gratitude with inspiration because they both stimulate good feelings. Inspiration may be defined as that which stimulates the mind or feelings of creativity or activity. When inspired, I'm more apt to take action to achieve something creative or for the common good. When I say "look for inspiration," I'm suggesting you look beyond yourself to intuition, a person, a Higher Power, or even a

---

38. Emmons, R. A. and M. E. McCullough, eds. *The Psychology of Gratitude.* London, Gr. Brit.: Oxford UP, 2004.

miracle of nature to help you move toward openness and away from self-limiting thoughts. When you listen to your intuition or wiser self, you can often find inspiration. When we are open, we can turn to a source of guidance, wisdom, and serendipity. Inspiration can be a new or better way of approaching something. It is getting away from set patterns and exploring new avenues where our creativity is unleashed. Inspiration allows us to step outside the box, innovate, and create new possibilities.

Try an experiment of loving your life and being grateful for all you have. We forget to appreciate the abundance, which becomes clear when we see others who do not have enough food, friends, money, or a home. Following are actions you can take to cultivate gratitude and love of life.

- » Allow yourself to focus on what you do have; experience gratefulness and be open to inspiration.
- » Be open to and expect synchronicity and creativity. Keep track of moments of inspiration and creative ideas.
- » Notice your habitual pattern. Do you focus more on what is missing or being grateful for what you have?
- » Recall the Taoist farmer who said, "Who knows what's good or bad?"
- » Look for the gift in what may seem like a setback or obstacle.
- » Practice noticing and commenting on what is going well. Practice seeing possibilities in situations and looking for connections. Expect to find creative solutions. Expect inspiration and new ideas to emerge.
- » Note or keep a gratitude journal where you identify three moments of gratitude and new ideas or connections that you experienced that day. Be sure you actually experience those moments of gratitude rather than just performing a rote recitation of what you appreciate. Expand your list. Look for small moments.

» Recall a friend, pet, loved one, or special place in nature for which you are grateful. Notice how you feel when you are in an open state of gratefulness. Allow yourself to sense that experience of making connections and hopefulness.

» Find a photo of a beautiful place such as a sunset or a beach where you naturally feel a sense of awe and appreciation in the moment. Have the picture on your phone or desk to remind you of those precious moments. Allow yourself to find that sense of awe in the current moments.

» Have a mental album of moments you are grateful for. I can easily recall beautiful moments with friends, family, and nature. Remembering these moments reminds me to capture similar memories.

» Study innovation and how others have developed creative solutions.

» Recall difficult times you have overcome and reflect on what you learned and what you are grateful for.

» Read poems and other inspiring quotes and materials that remind you to be thankful and in the moment.

» Change your internal language from "I can't" or "I don't know" to "What if..?"

» Create reminders to support you in reflecting on what you are grateful for. Engage others in reminding you and talking about gratitude.

» Make the commitment to practice gratitude often. Research shows that making a vow to express gratitude supports the practice. Post your commitment where you will see it often.

» Focus on the good things others have done for you and express thanks and gratitude. Remember to write heartfelt notes of gratitude to people in your life.

» Reflect on the shortness of life and appreciate all the little things that provide comfort and joy in your life.

- Write a letter of gratitude to someone you have not adequately thanked. Share how their support made a difference to you. Research suggests that if you read the note to the person, you and they will experience positivity that will last for weeks.
- Counter negative things you notice with what is going well.
- Take care of yourself. It is hard to focus on what you are grateful for when you are tired and low on energy. Take care of your energy with healthy food, adequate sleep, and time for physical activity and relaxation.
- Savor the beautiful and joyful moments. Notice beauty in nature and your surroundings.
- Use the language of gratefulness such as: fortunate, gifts, blessings, and abundance.
- Expect inspiration and new insights in your life.
- Brainstorm as many ideas as possible without judgment when considering options for a challenge. Notice what is promising about each option. Make evaluation a separate step in the process. Look for innovation.
- Read inspirational essays and books to expand your sense of awe.
- Ask open-ended questions such as "What if...?" expecting new ideas to emerge.
- Experiment and try new things such as taking different routes, listening to unfamiliar music, and exploring new authors and speakers to open yourself to new ideas and inspiration. Be grateful for further findings and expect insight.
- Immerse yourself in nature, colors, music, and movement to shake things up and expect inspiration. Unfocused attention allows inspiration and creativity.
- Explore spiritual practices and read inspirational writings.

- » Practice guided visualization to explore different perspectives. You might ponder how someone you admire would handle a situation. Be grateful for this ability.
- » Many spiritual traditions believe prayers of gratitude are the most potent form of prayer. Offer your prayer.
- » Look up and ask yourself, "Am I grateful and open to being inspired?"

Be Connected and Supported

Be connected—receive and give support; connect with yourself, others, your environment and purpose [notice and touch your back and envision a community of support behind you]

"To keep your resolve, surround yourself with those who want you to succeed—and who are also on a path of practice. Agree on shared and individual behaviors that

reinforce your mutual support. The authors of Influencer found that it is the only way to permanently change."

— Kare Anderson

Connectedness may be defined as a feeling of belonging—a sense of relatedness to self, others, and the larger world. Thus far, we've talked about being grounded, optimistic, and grateful, each of which are stances that support us in being safe in our environment. Being connected recognizes the value of relationships as a means of support. That is, regardless of how alone or vulnerable we might feel, just imagining the connection and support of others and of ourselves can strengthen our resolve and give us the "backing" we need to stay open.

To assume we have support behind us—even when it is not readily apparent—is a way of feeling connected. I imagine someone "has my back" or is a backup. Then I am open to such support. It gives me the courage to stay open, despite my vulnerability. What if we believed that support was available for us to realize our goals? How would that belief and expectation influence our day-to-day life? Holding the view that support is available and working for others' benefit can become a self-fulfilling prophecy.

Self-awareness helps us recognize the value of connection and support. We come to realize we are not meant to function in isolation. When we know we are worthy of care and respect in our hearts, we can assume support is there for us. Similarly, when we notice we need help, we also become aware of how much others need our support.

Studies show that social connection is correlated with a 50 percent increase in longevity.[39] Strong relationships actually boost our immune systems. A lack of social connection leads to increases in anxiety and depression. Isolation is a more significant detriment to health than smoking, obesity, or high blood pressure. Social connection affects social, emotional, and physical wellbeing.[40]

---

39. Holt-Lunstad, J., Smith, T. B., and Layton, J. B. "Social Relationships and Mortality Risk: A Meta-Analytic Review." *PLoS Med* 7.7 (2010): e1000316. https:/doi.org/1371/journal.pmed.1000316.
40. House, J. S., Landis, K. R., and Umberson, D. "Social Relationships and Health." *Science.* 241.4865 (1988): 540-545.

Connecting with your mission, values, and purpose provides strength. I see my mission as supporting leaders in connecting with themselves, others, and the broader environment to enjoy life and make the world better. This awareness gives me strength and supports me in making decisions. I envision creating a difference and have a sense that "we are in this together." The Arbinger Institute, in its book *Outward Mindset*, emphasizes the critical difference between those who focus on the best interest of others and the organization's goals rather than just self-interest. Kare Anderson,[41] in her books on mutuality and her TEDx Berkeley talk "Redefine Your Life Around Mutuality," emphasizes that a key to a meaningful and adventuresome life is our capacity to connect with diverse people and work for each other's benefit, growth, and wellbeing. We can accomplish more and something greater together than we can on our own. When our mindset shifts from me to we, new possibilities emerge. Looking for common ground and shared interests enables us to connect for good.

Many of us experience feeling alone, especially when we feel overwhelmed or sad. While we are each independent, we are also interdependent. We all need relationships where we share empathy and understanding, where others listen with compassionate curiosity. It is useful to trust that support is available and adopt the intention of supporting others.

I know I have often felt that I had to do things by myself and help would not be available. In reality, we are interconnected, and we all have a lot more support for our living than we realize. We could not eat if someone had not harvested the crops and someone else transported the food. Others packaged and made it available. We saw how much we rely on each other during the coronavirus pandemic. We are interdependent, and more support is available than we may believe.

I believe the world would be better for all if we each identified an area of need and applied our skills, talents, and resources. Surely others would benefit, and we benefit from devoting our time and energy to important causes. Even small actions such as helping elderly neighbors with groceries or getting their mail will contribute.

---

41. Anderson, K. *Mutuality Matters: How You Can Create More Opportunity, Adventure and Friendship with Others*. n.p., 2017.

Practices for Embodying an Open Stance / 119

I have been hosting meetings where people share their challenges. Others listen with empathy and offer their support with suggestions, referrals, and perspectives. These are heartwarming interactions where people experience community and our interconnectedness. Everyone benefits—those with the challenge and those giving. Commit to serve others and be open to receive support.[42] We really do need each other.

The research documented in the book *Connected* by Christakis and Fowler[43] shows that our mindset and behaviors are contagious. We are influenced by those around us in far more ways than we consciously realize. For example, Christakis and Fowler present compelling evidence that we affect one another's tastes, health, wealth, happiness, beliefs, and even weight. Make it your goal to befriend and support others and to think and speak more in terms of "we" and collaboration. Following are ways to collaborate effectively.

» At the end of the day, reflect on the meaningful moments in your life. Are you actualizing your values? Consider how to make experiences more meaningful.

» Savor the connections you experience with yourself, others, and the environment.

» Begin to notice the support in your life and appreciate those with whom you interact. Thank the cab driver, grocery clerk, work colleague, family member, and community members. All of these people influence our lives.

» Explore the interests of others. Identify common ground and shared interests. Make it a practice of looking for how you can support others.

» Make an effort to begin sentences with "we" or "you" rather than "I" or "mine."

» Invest in creating friendships and real connections in your life. Join a community or a class to meet people. Host gatherings to

---

42. Brown, S. L. et al. "Providing Social Support May Be More Beneficial Than Receiving It: Results from a Prospective Study of Mortality." *Psychological Science*. 14.4 (2003): 320-327.
43. Christakis, N. A. and Fowler, J. H. *Connected: The Surprising Power of Our Social Networks and How They Shape Our Lives*. New York: Back Bay Books, 2009.

develop relationships. Stay in touch with friends. Often at the end of life, people don't say they wish they had worked more. Instead, they regret not connecting with family, friends, and others more.

- » Find ways to support others and notice your experience.
- » Practice a kindness reflection that works for you and extend it to yourself, those close to you, acquaintances, and even foes. You may wish for safety/ease, joy, connection, and creativity. As you wish, allow yourself to experience each. Find a time for when to practice—as you begin work, when you brush your teeth, or when you wash your hands. Make it a habit. Research strongly supports the benefit of such a process. Those who adopt such a practice experience greater life satisfaction and better health along with many factors after just seven weeks of practice.
- » Make it your goal to support others and be open to receiving support.
- » Reflect on relationships that are meaningful to you. Contact people by email or write a note thanking the person.
- » Recall times when you did receive support and appreciated your mentors and others who were there for you in various ways.
- » Reflect on your values and what is most important to you; then clarify your purpose. Remind yourself often and make decisions that are aligned.
- » Assess the resources in your life, including friends, neighbors, colleagues, and family. Whom can you support and ask for support? People like to give support. When you allow someone to be of assistance, it often serves that person too. Make a list of whom you can ask for help and make specific requests. Make clear your request and be okay with hearing a no.
- » Allow yourself to receive support. If you are like me, you may need to build the muscle of asking and receiving. On the other

hand, you may need to develop the skill of giving to others. Both are important. Make it your goal to support others.

- » Ask others to join you to attain mutually-beneficial goals.
- » Look for opportunities to help others and do so without expectations. Being generous and of service will be meaningful.
- » Identify an area of interest such as children, prisoners, or the elderly, and study their needs; then create a project where you make a difference in someone's life.
- » Expand your view of family to encompass neighbors, colleagues, and others, including those who are diverse.
- » As you encounter people you don't know, envision them in your inner circle and expand your view of them and the two of you together. Remember to assume positive intent.
- » As you face decision points, connect with yourself and your values by asking how you are likely to feel about the choice at the end of your life.
- » Put your hand on your back and ask yourself: "Am I open to connecting with myself, others, and my environment, offering support and being supported?"

Be Open-Minded/Curious

Be open minded—curious and non-judgmental
[touch your head and be aware of thoughts]

"Those who cannot change their minds cannot change anything."
— George Bernard Shaw

A critical element of being open-minded is the impulse to be curious and open to learning without judgment. Being in a state of wonder supports continuous learning. When we can admit to ourselves and others that we don't know or understand something, we create space for deeper awareness.

While we like the feeling of being confident and having control, we can learn to revel in staying open and curious. Studies have found that curiosity is associated with less defensive reactions to stress and disagreement.

Carol Dweck's idea of a "growth mindset" shows the power of focusing on learning and growing instead of a "fixed mindset" where development is perceived as limited. When you believe that you and others have the potential to learn and grow, you are essentially open to the understanding that abilities and knowledge can be developed. Similarly, you will continually try to see a situation or person from a different perspective when you are curious. You will look for possible explanations for behaviors and actions. You will be open to learning more, recognizing that you do not see everything.

Curiosity allows us to adopt a sense of playfulness and an openness to discovering things we do not yet know. By being inquisitive with a sense of wonder, we are likely to be surprised and enjoy new understandings. We are more mentally alert when we are curious. We are likely to identify more opportunities.

Curiosity is often stymied when judgment kicks in—for example, in a conversation when you decide "I'm right, and he's wrong." We each seem to have a predominant signal, such as a tight stomach or a constriction in our throat when we are closed and judging. It requires a conscious effort to remain open and curious to learn more about others' perspectives. The point is to recognize your signal and pause before reacting. I remind myself to assume positive intent.

A key to being curious is asking compelling questions for which we don't know the answers. We can ask ourselves, "What can I learn and what can I discover about myself, another person, and/or the situation?" Here are some ways to build your curiosity muscle:

- » Make it a goal to be inquisitive. Ask, "Tell me more" with a genuine desire to learn. Act as if you are seeing the person or situation for the first time, or you've come from a different country or planet.

- » Allow yourself the space to say, "I wonder…" or "I am curious about…" and then genuinely expect to be surprised. You may want to take note of what you are learning in a reflection journal. Act as a curious anthropologist.

- » Mindfully listen deeply and attentively to others. Look people in the eye when speaking (when culturally appropriate). Listen to connect, rather than correct or win.

- » Remind yourself that your thoughts and assumptions are not always correct.

- » Engage in mindfulness practice for a few minutes each day to observe your thoughts—experiment with focusing on your breathing or focusing on a mantra. Be curious about the impact on you. This should strengthen your ability to operate more intentionally and positively.

- Journal what you are thinking and feeling to become more self-aware. Notice habitual patterns that emerge and their effect on you and others. For example, explore one of your patterns of consistently questioning a person's motives.

- Explore your narrative. Notice when you tell yourself things like: I know enough; I am the expert, and they don't have my experience. Instead, tell yourself things like: I can learn more; I don't know everything; I can learn from everyone.

- Remind yourself of the benefits you envision by being open-minded. For example, I will positively influence others; I will support a positive culture; I will make better decisions; my team and I will experience more innovation and creativity; I will share more connections and better relationships.

- Get feedback from others on how open to new ideas they perceive you are. Ask others what you can do to be more open-minded. Be open to others' perceptions.

- Continually seek perspectives that are different from your own.

- Ask yourself, "Would I rather be 'right' or successful, creative, influential, etc.?"

- Manage your time so you have time to reflect and are not so pressured that you don't have the space to listen or consider different views.

- Explore new subject areas. Allow yourself to be a learner and enjoy the sense of curiosity. These days, it is so easy to learn new things, meet new people, and explore. Make it your goal to try new things and note your experience. Read books, listen to podcasts, and watch movies that are different from what you normally consume. Expect to be surprised.

- Engage in activities where you experience a sense of openness. Perhaps you enjoy painting, gardening, walking in the park, or riding a bike. Find times when you leave behind your to-do lists and obligations and experience a time of rest and rejuvenation. For example, when I ride a bike or take a walk along the lake,

I feel open, unencumbered, and expansive. This is how I try to be when interacting with someone from a different perspective. Setting aside such times enables you to come back to the center and reconnect with openness and curiosity.

- » Challenge yourself. Explore an issue that is emotionally charged for you, such as gun availability or healthcare reform. Listen to a television or radio show with a different perspective and notice how you contract. Practice being open and listening to varying points of view. Try listening to Ted Talks and YouTube videos on topics that are new to you. Consciously look for different points of view and work to understand how they developed.

- » Engage in a conversation with someone who is unlike you (everyone). Ask someone with a different perspective how they came to their point of view. Stay curious and expect to learn.

- » Reflect on a time when you felt someone did something wrong to you or others. Try to consider the situation from that person's point of view and identify some reasons for their behavior and words.

- » Prepare ahead of time for difficult conversations or interactions. Consider role-playing with a coach or a friend and getting in an open state of mind.

- » When exploring ideas with others, build on their ideas by saying "yes/and." Share what you like about their ideas and build on it. Manage your judgment.

- » Explore a unique cultural experience, or a new part of the world. Expose yourself to new and different things regularly. Notice your response to differences, build the muscle of curiosity— stopping, stepping back from reacting, and becoming open to learning.

- » Practice looking for the good or positive in each interaction or situation. Catch yourself when you make negative attributions. Make it a game to find and identify the positive and notice the effect on you and others.

- » Listen, really listen, more than you speak. Study listening skills and practice active listening.
- » Ask questions for which you do not know the answers.
- » Put your hand to your head and ask yourself: "Am I open to being curious?"

Be Open-Hearted/Compassionate

Be open-hearted—compassionate and empathetic
[put your hand on your heart]

"Love and compassion are necessities, not luxuries. Without them humanity cannot survive."

—The Dalai Lama

> *"Dare to connect with your heart. You will be lifting not only yourself and those you love and care about, but also the world in which you live."*
> — Doc Childre, HeartMath Founder

When you are around someone who is open-hearted, you immediately feel it. They are typically warm, welcoming, non-judgmental, and approachable. To be open-hearted is slightly different than to be open-minded. The latter is about being open to thoughts and ideas. In contrast, open-hearted is about being open to feelings and emotions. When you are open-hearted, you are likely to be more vulnerable and less protected. You are [metaphorically] opening your heart to others.

Given the inevitable challenges of life, it is natural to protect ourselves and close our hearts to pain. However, when we wall ourselves off from the painful moments, we also squelch the fullness and joy possible.

When we open our hearts, we are loving, giving, and compassionate. Compassion is caring for others and recognizing that everyone experiences pain and suffering in some form. It is part of the human condition. When we are compassionate, we sense and acknowledge a person's emotions and offer kindness and empathy. We recognize our interconnection with others and are often compelled to demonstrate caring.

We also need to offer ourselves self-compassion. Kristin Neff, a leading expert on self-compassion, suggests being kind and gentle with ourselves and recognizing that being imperfect, failing, and experiencing life difficulties is inevitable. It helps to be non-judgmental and receptive. We observe our thoughts and feelings rather than suppress or deny them. Research by Neff and others indicates that more self-compassionate people tend to be healthier and more productive than those who are self-critical. Self-compassionate people feel more secure and experience more self-worth.[44]

Most of us seem to know how to have compassion for a friend who is going through a challenging time. We are kind and give empathy

---
44. Germer, C. K., and K. D. Neff. "Self-Compassion in Clinical Practice." *Journal of Clinical Psychology* 69.8 (2013): 856–867.

and support. Kristin Neff suggests that we treat ourselves like a friend and be kind and supportive to ourselves rather than self-critical and judgmental.

Compassion increases activity in the areas of the brain related to the release of dopamine and oxytocin. We feel compelled to take action to relieve suffering. Compassion generates positive emotions.

Compassion extends empathy to action that supports others. Compassionate people realize all humans want the same things, such as happiness, safety, health, and love. When we are compassionate, we are genuinely interested in another person's welfare.

Empathy can be seen as a way to demonstrate compassion or caring. Empathy is identifying specifically the emotions someone is experiencing and often feeling the emotions ourselves. Having an open heart and treating ourselves, others, and situations with compassion and understanding are at the center of an open heart. A basic human need is to be understood, and few of us receive enough empathy in our lives.

Empathy involves trying to understand how another person feels and what is important to them with kindness and without judgment. The ability to give and receive empathy is priceless. Often, people don't want to show empathy because they disagree with a person. Empathy understands a person's emotions, but it does not necessarily mean agreement.

It is helpful to name the emotion you believe a person is experiencing and then to pause a moment to allow them to check in to see what they are experiencing. The other person can then pay attention to their emotion and see whether the term identifies their feelings or needs. By supporting the person to identify their feelings, their passion and related energy are free to move. For example, we may say, "You seem disappointed," and then pause or "zip it up." Then the person can reflect and consider their emotion. Then they may confirm that they are disappointed or share that they are surprised. The key is that we are interested in and trying to identify the other person's emotions. The act of naming their feeling activates another part of their brain and allows their energy and emotion to shift. Generally, a little bit of empathy goes a long way.

In some cultures where it is essential to "save face," you can experience a person's frustration through your connection and facial expressions rather than naming their emotion. The other person will sense your compassion and care without your words.

When we open our hearts and give caring attention without judgment to another person and to ourselves, real transformation is possible. The power of heartfelt attention cannot be underestimated, and it is a skill worth developing. Offering empathy and showing compassion by caring for others is an essential ingredient for productive conversations. When we seek to understand another person's emotions and needs, we are positioned to find common ground and shared purpose with them. Agreements become attainable.

Again, self-compassion is essential to being open. The same process of giving empathy and care to others works when we pay attention to our emotions and identify what we are feeling. Just the act of being open, interested, and naming our feelings supports wellbeing. It allows us to become unstuck and open to new possibilities. We often experience multiple and conflicting emotions. For example, one part of us may want to move on, while another part is experiencing a fear of change. When we give ourselves empathy, we are more likely to relax and create the space needed for solutions to emerge.

Too often, we argue with emotions and say or think that we or others should not have such feelings. We need to manage our reactions and defensiveness and appreciate that we and others react based on our conditioning and background. Like the weather changes, our emotions continually change based on our thoughts, conditioning, and experiences.

Often, just being open-hearted and kind is enough to shift our experience or interaction. People can sense your open heart through your nonverbal cues and attentiveness.

An essential part of demonstrating compassion is forgiving others and ourselves. Given our past conditioning and our humanity, we all make mistakes. Sometimes, they are simple misunderstandings that arise from unhealthy patterns of interaction. For example, Keith was writing an email to an important client and did not respond to his spouse's questions. When she asked again, he raised his voice and yelled. In turn, his wife yelled back, and the cycle began anew. Each was angry with the other, and each blamed the other for being inconsiderate. Each needs to forgive him- or herself and the other person. Keith admitted that he was short-tempered because of his anxiety with a work project. His spouse admitted that she had hoped he would be available to discuss an issue with one of their children. One or both partners needed to catch their emotions and shift to being open. They needed to forgive themselves for being stressed and anxious and to forgive their partner for their reaction. Both had to stop their habitual pattern of yelling at one another. Both would benefit from taking responsibility for noting their emotions and cooling down.

Sometimes, trust breaches are more significant when betrayal, lying, and lack of accountability are involved. Even when other people hurt or wrong us, it is useful to find a way to forgive them and ourselves. That does not mean you will stay in a negative relationship. You can set boundaries, define respectful behavior, and forgive one another.

Practice being open-hearted to yourself, others, and your situation. Here are some ways to practice:

» Notice your moods and emotions. Build your emotional vocabulary, and without judgment, name your emotions. For example, "Something in me is angry" or "Something in me is irritated." When you do this, you acknowledge your emotions, and another part of your brain is activated. Your prefrontal cortex rational brain is active. It will enhance your self-regulation to just be with your many emotions. Also, noticing and accepting our emotions decreases the stress related to suppressing emotions.

» Imagine a child, pet, or someone with whom you are empathetic and open-hearted. Allow yourself to experience the warmth and your appreciation of the person or pet. Notice how you are feeling in your body. You can recall this openness to remind yourself how you would like to be compassionate with others and yourself.

- Put yourself in situations that support your compassion. See movies and read books to learn more about others' perspectives. Look for ways to appreciate where others are coming from and let them know you are trying to do so.

- Shift your attention from your thoughts or head to your heart. Imagine breathing through your heart. Notice your shift in perspective from this stance.

- Practice giving and receiving empathy with others to learn more about the influence that empathy can have. If possible, practice with others or in a workshop to receive feedback on how you give and receive empathy. Offering empathy is a skill you can develop.

- Try to embrace painful or difficult challenges rather than suppress or repress your emotions. Take a deep breath and acknowledge your feelings, such as worry, fear, or anxiety. Trust that your feelings are giving you clues of what you need and what is most important to you. For example, you worry about a project that may be confirming how vital excellence is for you. You can then examine if there are other ways this value is or can be satisfied.

- Make it a practice to listen to your heart to discern what you most want. See what emerges. Comfort yourself by perhaps putting your hand on your heart and saying something soothing like, "This is challenging." This is listening to yourself with compassion.

- Appreciate beauty with an open heart. Find beauty in nature, people, art, music, sounds, poetry, food, etc.

- Create time for solitude to be still and connect with your heart. Become aware of your inner critic with its many "shoulds." Treat this inner voice with kindness and understanding. Question how true your "should" statement is and create a new affirmation.

» Note people or situations in which you naturally feel compassion. For example, I have a natural empathy for young children and those in difficult circumstances. I adopted my daughter and have compassion for children without parents. Notice your heart area and how you feel when you focus on someone or a particular group of people. Imagine carrying that compassion to others with whom you interact.

» Make it your goal to understand what is going on for people who may bother you. We are all experiencing challenges and insecurities. We cannot see what is happening in an individual's life. Perhaps the person's partner is ill, and they are short on sleep. Maybe they are worried about the company's viability and not paying attention to something you deem necessary. Noticing your awareness when learning about the background of a situation shifts your view.

» Practice loving-kindness meditation. Research by positive psychologists such as Barbara Frederickson[45] shows the benefit of visualizing sending kindness and support to yourself, your friends and family, your coworkers, and then those you may not favor. This helps us to see how we are all connected and supports health and wellbeing. The loving-kindness exercise involves focusing benevolent energy toward yourself and others. First, you relax and imagine peace and wellness toward yourself. You repeat such phrases as: "May I be happy. May I be safe. May I be vibrant and active, and may I give and receive appreciation today." After you focus on yourself, you can concentrate on another person and say the same sentiments such as "May they be happy. May they be safe. May they be healthy and strong, and may they experience appreciation today." You can then widen your circle to include family members, friends, and colleagues. You can extend the thoughts and well-wishes to others in the world and even those with whom you have had negative relationships. After seven weeks of practice, participants were found to have increased life

---

45. Fredrickson, B. L. *The Love 2.0: Finding Happiness and Health in Moments of Connection.* New York, NY: Hudson Street Press, 2013.

satisfaction, reduced depressive symptoms, and decreased bias toward others.

» Accept that you have had pain and negative experiences in your life. Visualize softening the wall around your heart to be open to more connections. Brené Brown, Researcher and author of *Daring Greatly*, refers to this as heart armor.

» Make it a goal to practice unconditional love toward yourself. Embrace and love the younger versions of yourself or your essence.

» Remember that we can't see what others are experiencing or readily perceive their background conditioning. Find compassion for each person you meet.

» Make it a daily practice to forgive others who hurt or upset you. Also, forgive yourself. You will benefit more from forgiving more than the other person.

» Note that others are suffering and have desires and needs, "just like me." Look for how we share interests and aspirations with others. We are in this together.

» Many heart-opening yoga poses are also an effective way to open your body, mind, and heart.

» Put your hand on your heart and ask yourself: "Am I open to being compassionate with myself, others, and situations?"

Be Open-Centered/Courageous

Be open-centered—courageous/vulnerable and take risks
[put your hand on your belly]

"Vulnerability is the birthplace of love, belonging, joy, courage, empathy, and creativity. It is the source of hope, empathy, accountability and authenticity."

— Brené Brown

Our gut contains a lesser-known nervous system, sometimes known as our "second brain." The connection between our two brains plays a crucial role in our overall health. Being open-centered and aware of your gut-brain connection supports your relationship with self and others.

We rarely think about being open in our core center or belly. What does it mean to be open-centered? Recent research suggests we have innate intelligence not only in our head and heart but also in our gut. People who check in with their guts are seen as more adaptable. In his book *The Second Brain*, Michael Gershon[46] describes how the gut has 100 million neurons and uses all the neurotransmitters in the brain.

Leaders who check in with their guts are seen as more adaptable. Our bellies give us clues to when we are reacting based on fear or courage. In a blockbuster TED talk on vulnerability, Brené Brown emphasizes the value of being vulnerable and also of taking risks in our interactions.

---

46. Gershon, Michael D. *The Second Brain: A Groundbreaking New Understanding of Nervous Disorders of the Stomach and Intestine.* New York, NY: HarperCollins Publishers, 1999.

Taking risks and being vulnerable support us in connecting with ourselves and others and being innovative. The courage to step outside of our comfort zones is required to be successful in our volatile and uncertain world. Most of us have had the experience of feeling alive when we are taking creative risks.

Being vulnerable is not easy and takes intention. Recall that it is our nature to protect ourselves; fear and the desire to control are natural. We often spend too much energy trying to be perfect and working to ensure our safety. Brené Brown comments, "Perfect and bulletproof are seductive, but they don't exist in human experience."[47] We all are being called to be authentic and vulnerable and take risks in the face of uncertainty. None of us knows what is going to happen. We naturally experience emotional exposure when we are vulnerable. To be successful, we need to listen to our gut (use our intuition) and pay attention to facts. When we take stock of both our center and the facts, we can decide to proceed, even without all the information we would wish to have. Yes, we will make mistakes, but then we need to forgive ourselves and move on. If you insist on trying to be perfect, you will stunt your growth and that of others.

We need to manage our tendency to compare and judge ourselves and others and learn how to be "good enough" leaders, parents, and humans. Yes, we will experience disappointment and failure, yet we need to accept those as part of the human experience.

Yes, this means we need to forgive others, too, when they disappoint and hurt us. We all are seeing and experiencing life differently based on our conditioning and background experiences. We need to recognize that when people are closed and their nervous systems are not regulated, they don't have access to their neocortex and undoubtedly will say and do things that may not serve them or us. We need to support people in being open. We can each focus on being open ourselves and positively influencing others.

The benefit of being vulnerable and creating an environment for others to do the same is greater intimacy and connection. Brené Brown found in her research that people who are courageous in sensitive

---

47. Brown, Brené. *Daring Greatly: How the Courage to Be Vulnerable Transforms the Way We Live, Love and Lead.* New York, NY: Avery, 2015.

situations experience a sense of worthiness and a feeling of being enough. Managing our fear, being open to sharing ourselves, and taking risks is an essential aspect of an open mindset.

Remember the stories of those on the hero's journey? Each hero confronts his fear, becomes vulnerable, and takes risks to conquer the dragon or another dilemma to achieve his goal.

With an open mindset, we accept that we don't know everything and are not in control. This frees us to learn and explore more. We are free to try things and learn from mistakes. Here are some ways to develop an open-center:

- » Make it a practice to recognize your fear; be open and vulnerable, and take risks. Allow yourself to make mistakes, and forgive yourself and others. It is better to try and fail than never to try.

- » Share what is going on for you with others. Share what you are noticing, the emotions and sensations you are experiencing and your impulses.

- » Recall times when you were courageous, took risks, and followed your gut. How was it for you to do so?

- » Observe and study others who have been both vulnerable and courageous. Notice the journeys of heroes. Identify a role model to encourage you to try new things, start new projects, and build new relationships. All heroes face challenges and are courageous in their journeys to success. Recognize that there will be false starts and failures along the way. How do you learn from "failures"?

- » Become aware of what supports your courageousness and that of others. Perhaps it is whom you interact with and what you read, and how you talk to yourself and others.

- » Practice putting your attention a few inches below your navel and perceiving things from this place. Martial arts traditions such as Aikido call this area the Hara and emphasize the power of moving from this center of gravity. What do you notice from this perspective?

Practices for Embodying an Open Stance / 137

» Recognize that you do not see the whole picture and be okay with that. See life as a journey, and be kind to yourself and others.

» Try to visualize your mind as the sky and your emotions, both positive and negative, as clouds passing by. Your feelings are not determining your actions.

» Challenge yourself to step out of your comfort zone with small experiments to try new things and share your emotions and perspective. For example, speak up at a meeting and eventually give a presentation before a large group. Trust that you can build the muscle of courage.

» Reframe failures as opportunities for learning and appreciate the risks you have taken.

» Maintain your integrity. Tell the truth and do not compromise yourself. Recall Keshavan Nair's "With courage, you will dare to take risks, have the strength to be compassionate, and the wisdom to be humble. Courage is the foundation of integrity."

» Find and get to know courageous role models.

» "Follow your bliss" as famed mythologist Joseph Campbell recommended. Listen to what excites you and take action in this direction even if you don't feel entirely ready.

» Take time to define your purpose or calling and allow this vision to inspire you.

» Put your hand on your center and ask yourself: "Am I open to being courageous, being vulnerable, and taking risks?"

Be Open-Handed—Kind Actions

Be Open-Handed—kind action, welcoming, accepting, non-judgmental and respectful [open your hands].

"The cool thing is that jazz is really a wonderful example of the great characteristics of Buddhism and the great characteristics of the human spirit. Because in jazz we

share, we listen to each other, we are creating in the moment. At our best, we're non-judgmental."

— Herbie Hancock

By being open-handed, I envision taking kind and impactful actions. We can ask ourselves, "What will be a kind action to support being open?" Often, it will be welcoming, non-judgmental, and respectful of yourself and others. Accept that people have different backgrounds and experiences, and most of the time they are doing the best they can. Focus on being inclusive and creating welcoming environments. Take full responsibility for your feelings and actions and for creating a welcoming environment.

An extensive study of leadership behavior and best practices across industries found that the most effective leaders demonstrated a single characteristic: kindness.[48] Work on becoming aware of your biases. Look for what is positive. Advocate kindness and respect for differences. Recognize that we have more in common than we do differences.

---
48. Baker, William and Michael O'Malley. *Leading with Kindness.* New York, NY: AMACOM, 2008.

Recognize that people have different definitions of respect. Work to identify what people need to feel respected and then clarify your intention of being respectful. We all think we are respectful. However, after working in many multicultural organizations, I have learned that we often have very different needs and definitions of respect. One manager expects people to wait outside of their door until they complete a meeting before entering, even if they are quite a bit behind schedule. Another leader in the same organization expects people to arrive on time and interrupt a meeting to help keep them on schedule. Where do we learn what respectful behavior is? We know from our early caregivers what it means to be on time and behave in different situations. These rules become unconscious, and just the way we should act. The various definitions are challenging in families, organizations, and environments where we have had different conditioning. Of course, if we don't feel respected, trust deteriorates and it is hard to create agreements together. Lack of trust often leads to a lack of psychological safety and polarization where sides are formed against each other. Unfortunately, polarization leads to stronger emotions of right and wrong. What is needed are open-minded conversations with empathy and shared insights and understanding.

When we consciously focus on creating open, collaborative, and welcoming environments, we are better positioned to engage in conversations to develop results and achieve potential. We each can concentrate on being welcoming in our language and inclusive of others by having open hearts. We need to focus consciously on building and maintaining trust. I share a process for being open-minded and engaging in positive and productive relationships in my book *OASIS Conversations: Leading with an Open Mindset to Maximize Potential.*[49]

Just as we need to extend a respectful hand of welcome to others, we benefit by spreading the same welcoming acceptance to the different parts of ourselves. We have all experienced an inner critic and elements like a perfectionist or a lazy aspect of ourselves that we judge harshly. We can notice and accept these different aspects that likely served us

---

49. Van Eron, Ann. *OASIS Conversations: Leading with an Open Mindset to Maximize Potential.* Chicago, IL: Open View Press. 2016. www.OASISConversations.com.

at another time and now may be conditioned behaviors. For example, it may have helped you not to engage much with others since that was the safest thing in your family of origin. The same practice may be causing more pain than benefit now. It may be kind of you to engage more with colleagues to create a positive collaborative work environment. When we can be open to all aspects of ourselves, we can experience a sense of spaciousness and have more energy.

Be open to discerning what actions we can take to create welcoming environments where we connect with ourselves, others, and our situations. When we are being open, we are positioned to make a difference in the world and others' lives. Here are some open stance actions to create better environments for everyone:

- Make it a goal to do one kind thing for another person each day.
- Express appreciation for who others are and what they do.
- Embody compassion and take actions that are supportive of others.
- Identify ways you will contribute to making your family, community, and workplace better. Find what is yours to do. Even small actions can make a difference.
- Notice the impact of your actions on the health of others and systems.
- Expect your actions to contribute toward a cause you care about. Even spreading kindness to those you interact with will have a ripple effect.
- Volunteer to support someone who is in need.
- Engage in self-care and do one kind thing for yourself. Envision this kindness spreading.
- Take care of yourself and find how you can best contribute using your insight, talent, and skills.
- Remember to assume positive intent. Recall that intention does not equal impact. Be curious and pay attention to the impact you are making.

- » Focus on being expansive rather than contracted. Catch yourself when you feel grumpy or judgmental; be kind to yourself, and work on being open to others.
- » Identify people whom you believe are welcoming, inclusive, and open-minded. Imagine how they would handle a situation. Explore what helps them to be open, and use them as role models.
- » Engage in conversations about what respectful behavior is to others in your family, organizations, and community. Check-in from time to time to see whether people are experiencing respect and trust. Develop a list of norms or expectations with your team of respectful behaviors that will support the team's effectiveness. Support conversations about the experience of respect.
- » Learn about different cultures and work to understand essential behavior that is important to individuals and groups.
- » Speak openly about your intention of supporting diverse and inclusive environments.
- » Work to invite diverse individuals into your home, workplace, and community. Foster friendships and healthy relationships.
- » Notice your judgment when you encounter differences and work on shifting to being open.
- » Accept the different parts of yourself and welcome your conflicting needs.
- » Reflect on how you can be supportive to others.
- » Reach out your hands and ask: "Am I open to being kind, respectful, non-judgmental, and welcoming?"

Putting It Together: The Joy of Being Open

"A mind is like a parachute.
It doesn't work if it is not open."

— Frank Zappa

Open Stance Postures

As a way of being open and building an open mindset, make it a practice to visualize each of these stances and check whether you are open or closed. You can use your body as a way to recall the various postures of an open mindset quickly. You can imagine walking through the components around your body and then, beginning with the open-minded/curious stance, proceed down to embody the four other stances.

Visualize and experience being open in the following areas. See the image below.

» Be Grounded and Appreciate What Is—Be present in the moment; breathe [feel your feet on the ground; appreciate what is]

Practices for Embodying an Open Stance / 143

- » Be Optimistic about What Is Unfolding—Imagine a positive outcome to what is unfolding [look forward and envision a favorable future]
- » Be Grateful and Open to Inspiration—Experience thankfulness, trust intuition, inspiration, and creativity [look up]
- » Be Connected—Receive and give support; connect with yourself, others, the environment, and your purpose [notice and touch your back and envision a community of interconnections and support behind you]
- » Be Open-Minded—Curious/non-judgmental [touch your head and be aware of thoughts]
- » Be Open-Hearted—Compassionate/empathetic [put your hand on your heart]
- » Be Open-Centered—Courageous/vulnerable [put your hand on your belly]
- » Be Open-Handed—Kind actions, welcoming, accepting, non-judgmental, and respectful [open your hands]

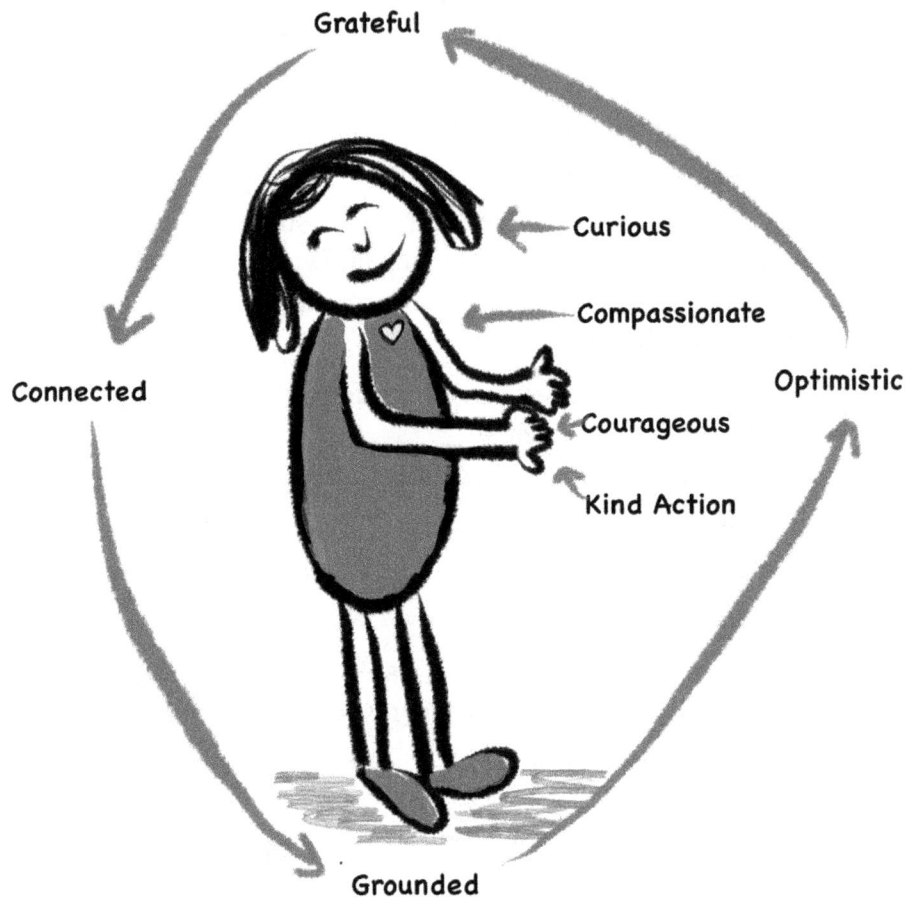

As you scan and reflect on each of these stances of being open, ask yourself, "Am I open or closed?" For example, "Am I experiencing being grounded or not?" Then, course-correct. You can refocus and take action to be in your body and to sense being grounded.

You can ask yourself, "Am I open-minded and curious?" If you are, great! If not, assess your thoughts, emotions, and background. Perhaps you are not curious because you sense that your colleague is betraying you, and you "know" you are right. This is your signal to stop before reacting. Step back and cool down. Breathe and recall that you "don't know what you don't know," and you intend to be open. Appreciate that your desire to be included represents your basic human need to be included. Give yourself some time to cool down and get some empathy from a friend and hear different perspectives. Perhaps a colleague informs you that there will be several meetings on the topic and the group has been divided to allow real dialogue. You see the situation differently, relax a bit, and are ready to ask your colleague about the meeting invitations. You are now open, can put aside your judgment, and can focus on learning more. If you find out that your colleague has indeed betrayed you, then you can have a conversation or take another course of action. Just stopping and becoming open and exploring will give you more possibilities than just reacting and then needing to clean up your reaction later.

If you find yourself not expecting support or not wanting to give support, again, this is a clue that you can assess what is going on for you. You may realize you need to ask more specifically for the help you need.

When you can assess your openness with the different dimensions of the Open Stance Postures, you will know what you need. It may be useful to ask a friend to listen and give you empathy as you explore your concern. Don't feel you will need to focus on each of the postures to be open. Make it your intention to be open to yourself, others, and your environment.

Through your intention of being open and through reflection, you will move more quickly from reaction and contraction to openness, responsiveness, and possibility. You will experience more insight, connection, opportunities, and joy. When we are grounded, open to the present moment, optimistic about what is emerging, grateful, and connected, we feel joyful to be alive. When we add curiosity, compassion, courageousness, and kindness, we genuinely connect with the joy of being human.

Open Stance / 146

    I believe this skill will support you in being successful in our multicultural, fast-paced, and rapidly changing, challenging world. When you focus on being open, you experience resilience, wellbeing, and are positioned to thrive. One way you can make a difference is to focus and build the neural pathways of an open stance and strengthen your mental fitness. Remember that emotions are contagious, so when you focus on being open, you naturally influence others to be open. What a difference your openness and joy can make. Recall the opening story of this book where Sarah noticed her negative relative and shifted to being open and ensuring the gathering was a success. We each have the power to influence those around us.

    As you practice being open, you will notice more readily when others are not open. It will help you focus on creating an open environment before working on solving issues or creating agreements. One sure way to do so is to continue to be open and not defensive. You can give the other person or people empathy and understanding. Share your intention of learning more and being curious. Acknowledge that you cannot see the whole picture, and wish to understand. Creating an open environment is essential to being an effective leader and influencer. You can find more ways to co-create solutions in my book, *OASIS Conversations: Leading with an Open Mindset to Maximize Potential.*

I encourage you to regularly revisit your commitment to being open and practice recalling the stances of being open as a daily ritual. Continue to ask yourself, "Are you open or closed?" Use the mental fitness process of Stopping, Stepping Back, Cooling Down, and Shifting to being open.

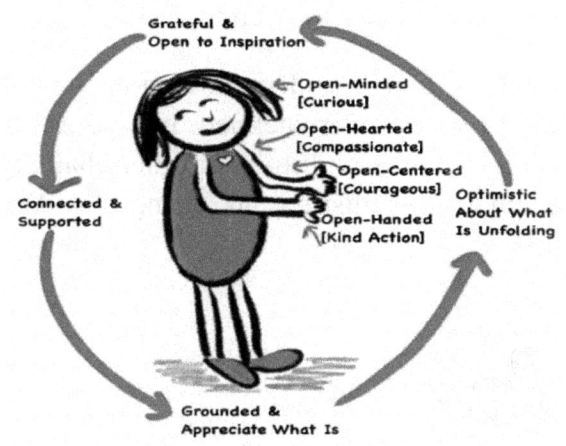

Part Four
Taking Action from an Open Stance

What the World Needs Now

"When a ship is in harbour and moored, it is safe, there can be no doubt. But that is not what great ships are built for.... Ours is not the task of fixing the entire world all at once, but stretching out to mend the part of the world that is within our reach.... One of the most calming powerful actions you can do to intervene in a stormy world is to stand up and show your soul. Struggling souls catch light from other souls who are fully lit and willing to show it."

— Clarissa Pinkola Estes

IT IS UNDOUBTEDLY A CHALLENGING time in the world with the pandemic, an economic crisis, social and racial inequities, political differences, climate change disruption, and overall polarization. People understandably report feeling tired and overwhelmed. Individuals are suffering from isolation, job loss, and a multitude of other challenges. According to experts like Jim Collins, disruptions, changes, and uncertainty may be the new norm.

This chaotic, uncertain time may also present a not-so-obvious opportunity where there is an opening for profound change in our institutions, our organizations, and our lives. The Margaret Mead quote comes to mind: "Never doubt that a small thoughtful, committed group of individuals can change the world. In fact, it's the only thing that ever has." We each can focus on making a difference in our own sphere of influence. If we each commit to being open and taking action, we will collectively make life better for all. From an open stance, we are positioned to make a difference. The question is: Are we willing to make that commitment, and can we find the support we need?

Each of us has the power to influence others. I am inspired by my organizational clients making life better for those they can influence. One leader uses his platform to shed light on inequities and work within his corporation to make systemic changes. Another client changed how her agency processes requests for improving roads and has made a renewed commitment to ensuring equity and fairness across neighborhoods.

On social media, we see examples every day of a person doing their part to support those in need, an elderly person tutoring young people who have trouble learning from home, or someone registering voters who have never voted before. People are using their talents and skills to make a difference. For example, some people are building desks for students who are studying at home. I hope you see examples of individuals affecting positive change in your community.

I have been reflecting on how I can best use my skills and expertise to contribute. It has always been my intention to support potential and assist people in taking an open stance and engaging in open conversations to create shared solutions. Of late, I am even more committed to exploring new ways of sharing my skills and facilitating challenging conversations. Because of the nature of my work, I have a slight twofold advantage. I see firsthand the hardships people are enduring, particularly within the workplace (i.e., loss of position/status, continuous cost-cutting, constant change, ongoing stress, overwhelming obstacles). At the same time, I also hear firsthand the stories of everyday heroism as individuals allow themselves to be vulnerable and open to creative and compassionate solutions. I am continually inspired when people identify projects and receive advice and support from peers. This affords me a perspective that is both hopeful and optimistic about the opportunity for positive change. I know it is possible. I witness it every day. I have evidence that when individuals commit to being open, they transform an environment. Leaders I work with report being open to colleagues, staff members, bosses, and stakeholders, and they see the power of others' intention. Where they once made negative assumptions and judgments, they come to understand different perspectives and opportunities. People share stories about how they are able to manage their judgments about others with different views, and through conversation, they create shared solutions and a climate of collaboration.

According to Gallup, just 33 percent of American workers are engaged in their jobs. Fifty-two percent say they are "just showing up," and 17 percent say they are "actively disengaged." Disengagement is typical in other countries too. A lot can be done to enhance work environments where people will be able to contribute more fully and achieve their potential. People do not feel valued or respected. What could happen if each team or organization member committed to taking action to create a more open and collaborative culture? For example, someone from the sales department could commit to building a relationship with someone in marketing. Small actions make a massive difference in creating a positive and productive environment. In one organization I worked with, everyone agreed the climate improved after discussing what each person considered to be respectful behavior. With this awareness, people began to assume positive intent and participate in ongoing conversations where they co-created positive solutions. Within a short period, all agreed that they enjoyed working together more. Engaging in conversations and making small gestures make a big difference.

Colleagues and I are facilitating Open Stance Project Circles in organizations. The highly interactive program integrates coaching, training, action-learning, and peer mentoring. Over several weeks, participants experience enhanced self-awareness, learn skills to embrace an open stance, build habits to support being open, and identify and experiment with projects to foster open, respectful, and engaging environments. Peers listen, challenge, and support one another in a live online session and coach one another between sessions. When people take action and support each other, so much can be achieved. Participants report meaningful interactions with more ease and faster, more creative, and satisfying resolution of conflicts. In addition, the collaborative environment of the circle creates a sense of community. This positivity is expanded to the larger organization and community.

We introduced such project circles in a professional association. Over time, after many open and honest conversations, we created an engaged and cohesive community. The intention to be open, and the subsequent supportive relationships that evolved, enabled the association to flourish. There is real power in making the intention to take an open stance and positively influence your family, workplace, and community.

From Me to We-Centric Focus

"As we learn how to reframe or shift our focus from fear-based thinking to embracing the future with energy and compassion for how to achieve success with others, we initiate a shift in our brains that moves us from pessimism to optimism—transforming habit patterns that hold us back into new patterns that catapult us into creating a Culture of WE."

— Judith Glasser

In addition to the very real pandemic that swept the world, we are experiencing an epidemic of isolation in organizations and communities. Long before we were encouraged to self-isolate for health reasons, people were feeling less connected as humans. We have been gradually losing sight of our commonalities and focusing on our differences, both politically and socially. People often tell me of the pain they experience in feeling on the "outside" and not respected for who they are, based on their real and perceived differences. We see a rising culture of fear, distrust, and polarization. People sense that others are closed to them, and they don't feel open to others. Some report that they feel invisible and like they don't belong.

Many sense an unraveling. Almost everyone I meet knows someone who has committed suicide or had a drug overdose; 47,000 Americans kill themselves each year, and 72,000 die from drug addiction. Of course, this pain tragically influences families and communities.

In the face of this kind of disruption and the many challenges we encounter, I reiterate my belief that the most vital skill needed today is to be open to what is possible. Shutting down and isolating ourselves even more is not the answer. The literature is replete with research documenting the negative consequences of the extremes of individualism we're experiencing today—and the seemingly long lost value of caring communities. For example, Otto Scharmer of the Presencing Institute suggests we need to shift from a focus on ego-system to eco-system and that we need to lead from the emerging future. He states:

> Bridging the gap between eco-system reality and ego-system awareness is the main challenge of leadership today. Decision-makers across the institutions of a system have to go on a joint journey from seeing only their own viewpoint (ego-awareness) to experiencing the system from the other players' perspective, particularly those who are most marginalized. The goal must be to co-sense, co-inspire, and co-create an emerging future for their system that values the wellbeing of all rather than just a few.[50]

---

50. Scharmer, Otto and Katrin Kaufer. *Leading from the Emerging Future: From Ego-System to Eco-System Economics*. San Francisco, CA: Berrett-Koehler, 2013.

I wonder, what could happen if more of us embraced an open stance and thought more about "we" rather than just "me"? Would we see the bigger picture and be more kind to our isolated neighbors in our workplaces and our communities?

David Brooks, the well-respected *New York Times* writer, suggests we are experiencing the excesses of hyper individualism and a focus on self-interest and self-expression. Perhaps it is time for the pendulum to shift in the direction of relationships and a focus on community and building cultures where openness and creating opportunities and wellbeing for all are valued.

The philosopher Martin Buber encourages us not to objectify each other. Rather than focus on "I-It," we focus on "I-thou" relationships where we appreciate each other's humanity.

There's a powerful African word called "ubuntu" that speaks to our shared humanity. It is about interconnectedness, empathy, and feeling kindness for one another. It is actually a philosophy, a way of acting in which a group's wellbeing is prioritized over the individual. All of our fellow human beings share a common bond, and through this bond, we discover our own humanity.

We know that when we are open to others, openness is contagious. By each of us setting the intention to be open, supporting others, and engaging in productive conversations, we can create more positive work and community cultures. The benefits have a rippling effect.

My executive clients will often say they are too busy to build and maintain relationships. They work long hours with significant commitments and pressures. They barely have enough time for family and essentials. I certainly can relate. Given the volatility and uncertainty we face these days, it feels like cultivating friendships and community can be last on the list. But should it be?

While we feel pressured, we must remember that relationships are what foster wellbeing and innovation. In his book *Tribe: On Homecoming and Belonging*, Sebastian Junger found that American soldiers in Afghanistan experienced a sense of wellbeing when living and working in community. The same soldiers experienced isolation after returning home. Many said they missed the connection. Junger makes the case that humans lived and worked together in close-knit social groups or tribes for hundreds of thousands of years. We value and thrive with connections of support. In our modern society, we have fewer chances of helping one another, and many feel divided and even depressed. These divisions have become even more extensive in recent years.

When disasters hit like floods, fires, and other calamities, we see people come together to help and support one another. After 9/11, people in New York City reported feeling more connected. The murder rate actually went down. We, as humans, are wired for collaboration and supporting each other. Research shows that wealthy urban women in North America experience more isolation and depression than rural women in Nigeria. While women in Nigeria are poorer, they have more social support and connections.

Many research studies are showing the health benefits of human connection. At the end of our lives, we reflect more on our relationships than other achievements.

I have built strong supportive relationships by joining groups of peers for reflection, support, and shared aspirations. We talk about professional issues that are challenging us. We offer suggestions and ask probing questions to enhance self-awareness. Typically by helping each other think through challenges, we gain insight into our own behaviors. I have built lasting friendships with these peers while we support one another in achieving our goals. We have learned a lot by sharing books and resources and have experienced the power of connection. I have also facilitated peer learning and coaching groups worldwide, and attendees always report that the relationships formed are meaningful and supportive. When we are vulnerable and listen intently, we experience our "we-ness" and commonality and feel less alone. Inevitably, I come away having learned as much as the people I'm coaching. Because of the diverse experiences and backgrounds, innovation and creativity are a natural outcome.

Make it your intention to be open and to spread that openness to your colleagues and community. Notice your experience and impact. Think about a group of friends or acquaintances who might share your commitment. Even if you just start with one or two, your community will inevitably grow over time. You will naturally want to spread the support you experience.

Commit to Action

"The most meaningful way to succeed is to help others succeed."

— Adam Grant

When we transition from an "I" to "We" mindset, it allows us to see each other from a very different perspective. We pay attention to our humanness as opposed to our differences. We are better able to understand folks who feel marginalized or misunderstood. Just by being open and listening wholeheartedly, we can empathize—and disagree respectfully. In my work, I've had countless conversations about systemic inequities and racism. These issues are real. I have supported many organizations in creating more inclusive cultures, and I have conducted hundreds of focus groups around race, gender, age, and other differences. I have coached many leaders and teams around these issues. From this work, I developed the OASIS Conversations process. I could see that we are not inclined to talk about challenging issues, nor are we skilled in it. It is easy to feel misunderstood or blamed. It is hard to admit we all play a part, intentionally or not, in allowing inequities to persist. We are each conditioned by our background experiences. While most of us don't intend to be biased, we are often unaware of the impact of our statements and actions. The OASIS process supports us in noticing our judgments and reactions and shifting to being open to engaging in meaningful conversations and co-creating shared solutions. See www.OASISConversations.com for more information.

There is a significant cost to individuals, organizations, and communities that lack dedication to openness, inclusion, and equity. They fail to see and take advantage of opportunities. The input of a broad spectrum of people of diverse backgrounds enriches our ideas and expands our thinking. When we see and relate to each other's humanity, we can move past seemingly irreconcilable differences. We are at a unique time in our history when there is significant opportunity. At the same time, there is uncertainty in many arenas. Will we commit to the kind of transformation that will be required? Only if we are willing to open our minds and hearts to one another.

First, to make that transformation happen, we need to educate ourselves, to deeply explore the stories of others who are not like us. Who are they? They are the people who have religious beliefs that seem odd to us; they are the young people who seem outlandish in their choice of dress and music, not to mention lifestyle choice; they are the people whose cultural norms don't seem to align with our own; they are the family members who have very different political beliefs; they are the politicians who don't seem to care. Finally, they are us, and we are them. We can't pretend to understand their experience by merely relating it to our own. Do we know what it feels like to be unable to catch a cab because of the color of our skin? Or can we know the fear a mother has when her black son is driving? Or what it's like to have to navigate the world from a wheelchair? Do we understand the shame of not being able to provide for our family? There are many resources to study and educate ourselves—books, films, articles, TED talks, church groups, and community diversity endeavors. Once you make the commitment to learn, you'll be amazed by what's available!

When we more fully understand our history and others' history and experiences, it will help us be more empathetic. We have all been impacted by our conditioning. We need to embrace our multiple differences and the unity we share.

Then we need to be emotionally intelligent. We need to be aware, not only of our own emotional triggers but attuned to others' emotional reactions. We need to recognize that what is emotionally challenging for others may not be for us. And vice-versa. We are each literally paying attention to different observable data. What is apparent to one person is literally not even visible to another. We each make our own unique assumptions and experience different emotions and judgments. In my work, I've often been called upon to help resolve conflicts between individuals and groups. The first thing that becomes apparent in any conflict setting worldwide is that we actually "see" things differently. Therefore, we don't hear what the other is saying.

When we are truly curious and begin to listen attentively to one another with the intent of being open and understanding, we actually start the transformation process. This is what being open-minded, being open-hearted, and taking an open stance is all about.

As we genuinely listen to one another, are vulnerable, and empathize with compassion, the solutions naturally emerge. These are the conversations necessary for our families, workplaces, and communities.

In addition, systemic efforts are needed to effect broader change in processes and structures to ensure equity. For example, we must work to elect politicians who share the vision for a more equitable future and who will change policies and practices locally, state-wide, and nationally to represent all their constituents. In our own workplaces, we must look for ways to influence policy changes that foster fairness, respect, community engagement, and inclusion. This might include human resource policies that prioritize fairness and compensation equity. We need to look for win/win solutions to ensure all benefit, rather than leave some feeling like they are invisible.

I appreciate that leaders in organizations are coming forth with commitments to invest energy and resources in creating more inclusive and collaborative cultures. Fortunately, there seems to be a growing awareness that the diversity of ideas can only come from the diversity of the people who present them. We need to honor and be open to creating opportunities for all.

We can each make a commitment to action. I will be facilitating groups where people support each other in being open-minded and taking measures to make a difference. We know real transformation will take time, effort, and discomfort. Nonetheless, this time of uncertainty may be the perfect time to create more openness, compassion, and collaboration in our lives.

Commit to one action today to be a part of the collective solution where people know that they matter and take effort to make the world better for all.

> *"The openness of our hearts and minds can be measured by how wide we draw the circle of what we call family."*
> — Mother Teresa

Choose a Project

> *"Openness isn't the end; it's the beginning."*
> — Margaret Heffernan

I encourage you to identify at least one way you can make a difference in your sphere. Ideally, you will join with colleagues to support one another in making the world a bit better.

One thing we can each do is set our intention to be open to others in our life at home, at work, and in our community. If we keep an optimistic, curious, and compassionate perspective, we will naturally influence others and inspire positive and productive relationships and an innovative environment. Remember that emotions are contagious. Recall Sarah's story of how she saved her spouse's big day by noticing her reaction to the negative relative. She was able to be aware, recall her intention, and shift to being open. Her open stance made a difference for all involved. If we each make such a move regularly, we can indeed make an impact.

Taking Action from an Open Stance / 161

There is no shortage of needs at the local level—in our families, neighborhoods, community organizations, schools, and government. There are also global challenges that require a lot of focus and effort. These include climate change, racial justice, health disparities, education differences, polarization on many issues, leadership development, poverty, food insecurity, technological challenges, post-disaster relief, community building, conflict resolution, etc. Many opportunities for societal change, as well as local change are awaiting us.

Review the Sustainable Development Goals[51] established by the United Nations to transform the world by 2030. The challenging goals include ending poverty and hunger and creating good health and wellbeing for all, providing clean water and quality education, offering affordable and clean energy, reducing inequalities, and building sustainable cities and communities with decent work and economic growth.

It is easy to feel overwhelmed with all the needs. However, we can each start small. Reflect on what draws your attention. Facilitator, author, and conflict resolution specialist Priya Parker tells of how her mother taught her to ask herself the following questions: "What is it I know how to do? Where is the need? How can I help?" Sounds simple? Yes, and this is also where we can get stuck. We have a tendency to

51. https://sdgs.un.org/goals

downplay what we know how to do (or our ability to learn it). We also tend to doubt that our gifts or what we "know" are of value to anyone else, and therefore, we stop ourselves before ever thoroughly assessing the need. And finally, we just bog down on the task of putting the two together and figuring out how we can help. We allow ourselves to get derailed before we even begin. Consider your skills and abilities and choose to take action where you and others will be strengthened.

For example, you can choose micro-actions such as greeting neighbors with a smile or offering to shop for an elderly or ill acquaintance. You can focus on an issue such as encouraging people to vote, plant trees, or provide funds to feed those in need. Perhaps you are inspired to work with youth or to develop aspiring leaders. Maybe you could share your knowledge about building a business, writing, or gardening. You could volunteer at your local food bank and learn firsthand about the needs of others.

Be open to what attracts you or something that concerns you. Begin to learn more about this issue or concern. Research shows that we have a greater sense of wellbeing when working toward a goal or purpose we care about. Besides, when you connect with others who care about similar issues, your connections also support wellbeing.

Identify Allies and Supporters

"Alone we can do so little, together we can do so much."
— Helen Keller

You don't need to take on projects by yourself. In fact, when you join with others who care about similar issues, you can magnify your impact. You can quickly learn what others are doing and build on each other's work and ideas.

The complexity of the challenges we face calls for partnering and supporting each other with initiatives. We are at a time where we can influence social change.

My colleague, Bruce Mabee, encourages people to be bold and reach out to others engaged in a similar mission to magnify what is possible. From an open stance, you can trust that possibilities will unfold. In her book, *Think Outside the Building*, renowned Harvard innovation expert Rosabeth Moss Kanter shares examples of professionals, executives, and entrepreneurs engaging in innovative projects to create positive change.

Kanter inspires us by sharing accounts of leaders who tackle real challenges such as climate change and economic insecurity. Leaders are reaching outside their corporations and joining businesses, government, and community sectors to deal with poor nutrition in inner cities while reducing food waste. She shares the story of a journalist turned entrepreneur who decreased social divides by giving social media users access to free local education and culture.

She also reminds us of Kanter's Law: "Everything can look like a failure in the middle." That's something valuable to remember as we embark on making a difference. Kanter proposes more than thinking "outside the box"—thinking "outside the building." She incites us to think broadly and form collaborations across individuals, organizations, and industries, and to mobilize more people to think bigger and differently about how to engage in positive action.

Co-creation requires a mindset shift. We need to be open and realize that we don't have all the answers. Who can these days? We need to be prepared to really listen and respect different perspectives and views. We need to co-create not only with our peers and team members; we need to genuinely listen to customers and those in other organizations and industries. We need to be looking for common ground and synergies across boundaries.

One example is Regional Talent Innovation Networks, where businesses, schools, and other community organizations join together to educate students and create a pipeline of workers to support their community. Those involved need to be open to different views to benefit the larger community. It takes openness and skill to co-create. My colleague, Ed Gordon, has devoted much of his career to forming coalitions across organizations, chambers of commerce, and schools to collectively develop programs to address the future shortage of skilled workers to prepare community members for future jobs that will ultimately benefit the businesses, citizens, and entire communities.

More organizations are considering how to be socially responsible citizens while still ensuring profits and being attuned to people's and the planet's needs. I am part of a community of leaders and coaches committed to creating a healthy and sustainable world focused on empowering quadruple bottom-line impact. The focus is on supporting people, the planet, profit, and purpose. We do this by starting small, initially within our own circle of influence, and expanding our endeavors by relying on one another's area of expertise to encourage us to think big!

In *Manifesto for a Moral Revolution*, Jacqueline Novogratz shares inspiring examples from the social enterprises she has supported to make a more just, inclusive, and sustainable world. She has sponsored bringing affordable education, healthcare, and clean energy to millions of people through her impact-investment and activism platform. She calls each of us to be leaders and to focus on making a real difference.

I recognize that the road ahead on many issues is complicated and messy. However, when we approach change from an open stance, we are more agile and flexible to learn and pivot where needed.

We can start with small experiments and reflect on what we learn. Then we can build on the findings and create scale where possible.

Open-minded conversation skills will serve us not only in surviving but thriving in our current environment. We can expand our focus from "me" to "we." How might our actions differ if we consider how to make things better for all?

Taking Action from an Open Stance / 165

Build Social Trust—Be Neighborly

"We live in a world in which we need to share responsibility. It's easy to say, 'It's not my child, not my community, not my world, not my problem.' Then there are those who see the need and respond. I consider those people my heroes."

— Fred Rogers

As noted, we are facing many challenges these days. An underlying issue is a decrease in social trust. Studies show there has been a decrease in trust in government, media, religion, and critical social institutions in America and elsewhere. While most see a decline in people being reliable and able to fulfill their obligations, according to Pew Research Center, 8 out of 10 Americans think that social trust can be repaired.

Where do we begin to rebuild trust in our institutions, as well as in each other? For starters, we can set our intention; that is, we can decide it is what we want to do. To repair social trust, we must start with ourselves and our own willingness to be vulnerable and open. It is one thing to decide; it is quite another to make a commitment. From there, one of the most natural extensions is to be open with a family member or a neighbor. With all of the needs we've talked about, there are so many reasons to reach out. We can commit to being a kind family member, a friendly neighbor, and/or a supportive community member. What could happen if we each used our skills, talents, and passion for consciously making a difference for our colleagues, community, and others? Simply acknowledging and listening to others, even when they have different views, could create a more positive environment. When we show that we care and desire peace, doors will open.

We are polarized by divergent political views and different areas of focus. However, we can come together as neighbors and work collectively on projects such as supporting youth or cleaning a park of litter and planting flowers. We can experience our common ground of wanting safe and life-enhancing communities—even when we have different world views.

Braver Angels is an organization that facilitates conversations between people with diverse political views. The participants are guided to listen fully and find common ground. Despite widely disparate views on issues, participants have recognized their common ground. Even friendships have been formed by people with very different lifestyles and beliefs. This kind of dialogue and recognition of the value of open dialogue is much needed, and the shared understanding is hopeful.[52]

Clearly, it is not easy to find answers that appeal to polarized positions. Barry Johnson's work proposes that we have difficult conversations where we share our different views and break down barriers by appreciating the polarities and addressing issues as dilemmas. We minimize the potential challenges of each side and find options that recognize our shared values.[53] He proposes a kind of both/and thinking in which there is always a middle ground.

David Brooks joined with the Aspen Institute to initiate the Weaver movement to repair the country's social fabric, which is frayed by

---

52. https://braverangels.org/
53. Johnson, Barry. *And: Making a Difference by Leveraging Polarity, Paradox or Dilemma, Volume One: Foundations.* Amherst, MA: HRD Press, 2020.

distrust, division, and exclusion.[54] "People are quietly working across America to end loneliness and isolation and weave inclusive communities." The organization collects inspiring stories of success and works to support the growing movement to enhance relationships. Some people build community in their neighborhoods and workplaces by working with youth, visiting the sick, or befriending the isolated. Brooks encourages people to join in "shifting our culture from hyper-individualism that is all about personal success, to relationalism that puts relationships at the center of our lives." I envision people choosing to take an open stance for such efforts.

We are facing many stresses, so we naturally become fatigued. Many are isolated and feel alone. Whether you start a global community development program or visit an elderly neighbor, we can each do our part to build positive and productive relationships and make life better for all. When you reach out, you will most likely receive more than you give. It is rewarding to experience a community connection. It will take all of us to contribute.

Benefits of Taking Action from an Open Stance

> *"It is not enough to be compassionate—you must act."*
> —The Dalai Lama

Doing something to make a difference—almost anything—can be energizing. From an open stance, you are likely to see and sense needs and opportunities. People report more meaning and satisfaction when they are focused on a positive purpose, supporting others, and making a difference. Research indicates that giving back to the community boosts happiness, health, and wellbeing. It may even extend your life.

> *"The best way to find yourself is to lose yourself in the service of others."*
> —Gandhi

Studies show that those who volunteer or give to others, such as working at a soup kitchen or coaching at-risk youth, are better equipped to manage stress, are healthier and less depressed, and experience

---
54. https://www.aspeninstitute.org/programs/weave-the-social-fabric-initiative/

increased life satisfaction. People who donate their time and energy to others are less lonely and experience more long-term health. A study found that Americans who described themselves as "very happy" volunteered at least 5.8 hours per month. Another study suggested that helping others may relieve chronic pain.

People who support others tend to have a greater sense of purpose and identify.[55]

Adam Grant, in his book *Give and Take*, demonstrated that givers who focus on what others need and are generous with their time, knowledge, energy, skills, ideas, and interactions with others are the most effective leaders. Givers can create a psychologically safe climate where everyone feels they can contribute. This type of environment supports learning and innovation.

When you feel good about supporting others and making a difference, you will also feel better about yourself. Working on projects and supporting others' needs, particularly those less fortunate, helps us put things in perspective with a greater context. We are likely to be more appreciative then of what we have than to focus on what we don't have.

---
55. https://www.mentalfloss.com/article/71964/7-scientific-benefits-helping-others

Engaging in projects and giving time, energy, and money to help others is contagious. Being kind and caring toward others can be infectious, inspiring others to do the same.

People who help others report a sense of joy. They often say they receive more than they give. It is believed that endorphins are released that allow a sense of calm and wellbeing that reduces stress. It is good and healthy to be engaged in some form of service. It connects us to ourselves, others, and the greater world.

I have met people I have become friends with while engaging in projects that are important to me. In addition, I have often been inspired by others' projects and volunteer actions. When we join with others to make a difference, we feel less isolated and experience a greater sense of community and belonging.

A colleague once called me a "citizen of the world." I embraced that identity. With the spread of the pandemic, we have seen how interdependent we all are. We all seek the same basic necessities of life. We are all experiencing suffering in some form, and there are many inequities. There are people without adequate water, people suffering from food uncertainty, and people who are depressed and alone. Some don't have jobs or proper internet connections. Some children aren't learning. Racial and gender inequities and polarization exist on many levels. If we each took small and large actions to rectify and create new opportunities, we could all benefit.

When you commit to being open-minded and take an open stance, consider yourself a global citizen. You can take a more expansive view of the world to make it more sustainable by your actions. "Global citizens are creative and proactive and able to think critically and make informed decisions about what is just, while at the same time showing respect for those around them and abroad."[56]

It is easy to become self-focused and emphasize academic and career "success." By expanding our focus on the wellbeing of our fellow beings and the world that sustains us, we can connect with a greater purpose and experience the joy of making a difference.

---

56. https://buildabroad.org/2017/02/17/global-citizen/

A simple internet search will reveal many resources readily available to find causes that will inspire you, and that can benefit from your energy and creativity.

The good news is that we can each take on projects to make a difference, no matter our age, stage of life, financial situation, or even health. We can each give and receive the benefits. Ideally, we will inspire others to do the same.

> *"The world changes according to the way people see it, and if you can alter, even by a millimeter, the way people look at reality, then you can change the world."*
> — James Baldwin

We Can Support Each Other

> *"We rise by lifting others."*
> — Robert Ingersoll

I have been hosting conversations with the goal of leaders supporting each other in being open and learning with each other. In small groups, one person shares a challenge they are facing and the kind of support that would be useful. For example, one person talked about how people are not being trained for jobs so a worker shortage will exist for many positions. He asked fellow leaders for suggestions on how he can communicate his concern more effectively and help communities educate workers for the needed roles. It will take companies, chambers of commerce, and others to join together. After he shared his concern and request, others asked questions, brainstormed, and offered suggestions. The leader left with a clearer view of his next steps, plus an introduction to a leader in another city who had organized such a program, and an introduction to someone at the Board of Education who is responsible for this issue.

Another leader, who was working on a complex project to support youth, shared her feelings of being overwhelmed with the organization of the process. She felt stressed as she tried to keep abreast of things. She asked for different perspectives on her challenge. She learned that she was not alone with such disorganization, which made her feel less judgmental toward herself. In addition, it became clear that she had tried various systems on the market to manage the project, and she really needed someone to support her in working with the way her mind works. Another person in the group knew of a coach in her area who had training in various project management systems. She left feeling understood with a perfect connection. She was more prepared to make a bigger difference using her talents and position.

Another person focused on a personal challenge she was having with colleagues and her frustration with interactions. She left the meeting with a whole new understanding of how her colleagues could be experiencing the situation. She felt understood by the group and had a new way of engaging with her colleagues. She felt more confident about succeeding with her project.

Each leader brought a different project or challenge to the group, and each left with greater understanding and clarity about their next step. All of the participants gained a deeper understanding of how they could effectively contribute. Most importantly, the leaders were open and vulnerable in sharing their concerns and were grateful to support one another and be supported. We are interconnected, so we need each other.

Many of the participants followed up with each other and made lasting connections. Participants said the experience was "transformational," "enlightening," "fulfilling," and "uplifting." The project circles benefit students, parents, neighbors, organizations, and a wide range of groups. We need to create opportunities to listen to one another, ask powerful questions, and genuinely support one another. We all benefit from the experience.

"Encourage, lift and strengthen one another. For the positive energy spread to one will be felt by all. For we are connected, one and all."

— Deborah Day

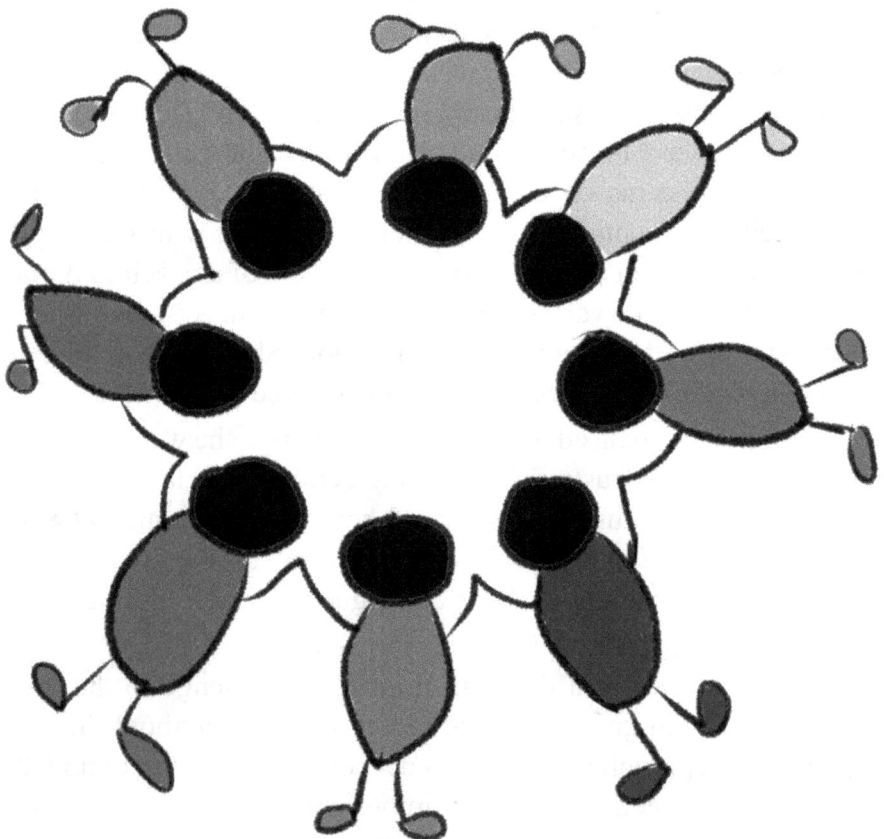

I hope you have made the commitment to be open-minded, adopt an open stance, and take action to make life a bit better for others. You don't have to travel this route alone. Find a coach, buddy, or a circle of people to join with, and then support one another.

I envision groups joining together to encourage each other to be open even in the face of uncertainty and constant change. Participants can share the practices they are using to be open and be accountable partners. In addition, team members can listen and be a resource to one another as each embarks on a project. As people progress with their projects, they can receive support, advice, feedback, and resources from each other. By using their talents and resources, participants will make the world a bit better and create connections and community with peers.

Participants can engage in dialogue about their experience of taking an open stance and support one another in building a practice to strengthen this muscle. Ideally, time could be spent reflecting on the elements of an open stance and how best to incorporate things like being curious, compassionate, courageous, grateful, optimistic, connected, respectful, and grounded in daily living. Then each person could share their passion and interest in contributing. Participants could provide feedback, suggestions, ideas, listening, support, and accountability.

It is a simple concept that could make a real difference. Not only will real community needs be addressed, but relationships across differences can be forged where people recognize and appreciate each other's humanity. Together we can build a better world for all.

Keep in Touch

"If you want to go fast, go alone. If you want to go far, go together!"
— Ubuntu Saying

When you are open, you will see many ways that you are making a difference.

I wish you the joy of being mentally fit and building the mental muscle to Shift to being open and creating many positive and productive relationships. Together, we can each do our part to make the world better for all.

    I hope this book has motivated you to take an open stance, shared a process for how to do so, and offered a plan for practicing. Please share what you notice and what you are learning with me and others.

    Visit www.Potentials.com for additional support.

    With gratitude,

    Ann Van Eron, PhD

    www.Potentials.com

    www.OASISConversations.com

Taking Action from an Open Stance

About the Author

Ann Van Eron, PhD, MCC, is CEO, founder and principal of Potentials, a global coaching and organization development consulting firm coaching leaders and teams all over the world for more than thirty years. She specializes in creating positive environments where people have open-minded and productive conversations that lead to unparalleled relationships, positive results, and wellbeing with leaders, teams, and organizations. Potentials has been engaged in supporting organization culture change, executive and team coaching, and providing leadership mindset and skill development.

Potentials specializes in:

» Increasing collaboration and innovation, even when people and agendas are in opposition

» Enhancing the skill set of executives and managers so they can lead and produce

» Supporting development of emotional and social intelligence to enhance relationships and outcomes

» Creating cultures of respect and open-minded conversations where teams succeed

» Navigating significant change effectively

» Resolving conflict and creating agreements
» Influencing openness to potential and possibility

Ann's clients include Fortune 100 corporations, nongovernmental organizations, healthcare agencies, and non-profit and privately held companies. Ann promotes leadership development and teaches managers how to be effective in coaching their teams. She assists organizations in creating cultures of respect and openness. She engages people in having mindful conversations for impact using her proven OASIS Conversation process. She is an author and speaker and offers training, coaching, and consulting to leaders, teams, organizations, and coaches. She is certified as a Master Coach and has a doctorate in Organizational Psychology from Columbia University. Ann is committed to assisting people in fulfilling their leadership potential and enjoying life.

Ann is devoted to inspiring leaders, coaches, and influencers in promoting an open mindset and open stance and engaging in positive and productive conversations for shared solutions. Her signature courses OASIS Conversations and Open Stance Leadership promote an open mindset and skills and have been shared in organizations such as the United Nations, CVS Health, New York-Presbyterian Hospital, the World Bank, and Ford Motor Company.

Ann lives in Chicago and enjoys photography, art, nature, traveling, and learning new things with colleagues, friends, and family. She is committed to being of service and making a difference.

Ann@Potentials.com
www.Potentials.com
www.OASISConversations.com
312-856-1155

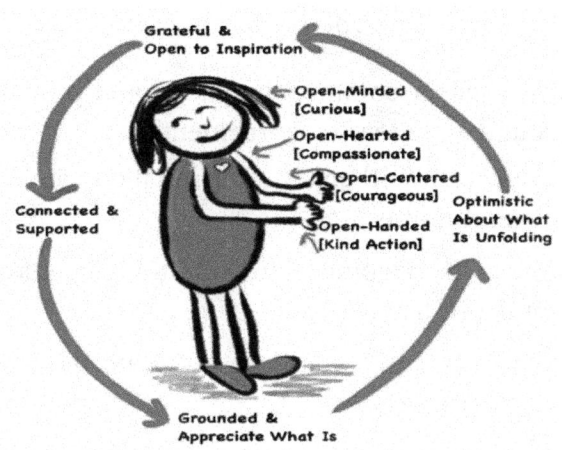

About Open Stance and OASIS Conversations Courses, Executive Coaching and Consulting

If you are looking for a dynamic coach and facilitator to guide you through the Open Stance and OASIS Conversation® processes with your team or organization, look no further than Ann Van Eron, the Open Stance and OASIS Conversation creator and her team of certified coaches and facilitators.

While OASIS focuses on how to have positive and productive conversations with people who have a different perspective, Open Stance focuses on our internal conversations and building the mental fitness of being open and resilient.

The Open Stance and OASIS Conversation processes have been tested all over the world with much success in such organizations as the United Nations, New York-Presbyterian Hospital, Cleveland Clinic, Caterpillar, GE Capital, Ford Motor Company, the World Bank, and other corporations.

When you hire Ann Van Eron to support your team in learning to be more open and find an oasis of agreement, you will find your workplace changing into a friendlier, more productive, and more understanding place within a short time.

OASIS Conversations and Open Stance Leadership produce results, improve relationships and wellbeing, save resources, enhance innovations, create efficiencies, spur rapid problem resolution, improve employee and customer engagement, and enable organizations and teams to share a common language and process for identifying common ground and creating agreements.

Benefits your team will enjoy by using the Open Stance and OASIS Conversations programs are:

- » Leaders will become more confident, centered, and present in the midst of turbulence.
- » Participants will be able to cultivate the emotions related to high performance.
- » Team members will be able to create positive climates and cultures that support open conversations for impact.
- » With the conversation skills and open mindset, leaders and others will experience more engagement, innovation, and real results.
- » Team members will be more emotionally and socially competent.

Besides workshops and webinars on Open Stance Leadership and OASIS Conversation skills, customized options tailored to your specific organization and needs are available. We interview team members in advance and facilitate unique experiences to support high-performing team development.

Also, personalized coaching is available. Learn your strengths and areas of opportunity for creating positive and productive interactions for unparalleled results.

Coaches and managers can choose to be certified in the Open Stance and OASIS Conversation process. See more details at www.OASISConversations.com and www.Potentials.com.

Also, consider booking Ann to speak at your next event on the importance of an open mindset and taking an open stance for greater resilience, wellbeing, and thriving. She will also share how to create OASIS Conversations for more positive and productive interactions.

You are also welcome to join an Open Stance Community to explore the practices and take action to make a difference. You can join an

OASIS Conversation Community to learn the OASIS Conversation process more fully.

To discover how Ann and her team of certified coaches and facilitators can help your organization and its members reach an oasis, contact her for a complimentary consultation:

Ann@Potentials.com
www.Potentials.com
www.OASISConversations.com
312-856-1155

www.ingramcontent.com/pod-product-compliance
Lightning Source LLC
Chambersburg PA
CBHW071447150426
43191CB00008B/1264